Step By Step
Bootstrap 3

A Quick Guide to
Responsive Web Development
Using Bootstrap 3

Riwanto Megosinarso

ISBN-13: 978-1499655629
ISBN-10: 1499655622

First Edition: May 2014
First Edition – Updated: September 2014

All information in this publication has been tested and verified to be reliable at
the time of publication. However, due to the possibility of human or mechanical
error, the publisher and the author do not guarantee the accuracy or
completeness of any information and is not responsible for any errors or
omissions or the results obtained from the use of such information. Readers
should be aware that links to external websites may have changed, moved or
disappeared between when this book is written and when it is read.

TABLE OF CONTENTS

1

INTRODUCTION

One of the big challenges in web development is maintaining the site's compatibility across devices and their various display sizes, from desktop computers to tablets and mobile phones.

The last thing we want is to have a website that looks good on a desktop but is painful to navigate on a small display, or looks great on a small screen but appears oddly tiny in the center of a large screen.

Ideally the site should have the ability to automatically reorganize itself to provide the optimal viewing experience, in accordance with the size of the display. In short, we want our website to be responsive.

This is where Bootstrap 3 comes in handy. It makes building responsive websites easier and quicker.

Why this book

Aimed at absolute beginners, this book will not require you to have any experience in HTML, CSS or JQuery. You will learn as you go along. It explains the subject matter in a step by step fashion, with plenty of examples and screenshots to illustrate the points.

All examples are downloadable. You can download, tweak and reuse them on your own project. You won't have to retype everything.

Who should NOT buy this book

If you are able to learn on your own by perusing the online documentation provided by Bootstrap, you do not need this book. Before you open your wallet, check out Bootstrap's official site and give it a go:

```
http://getbootstrap.com
```

What you will get from this book

In this book you will use Bootstrap to transform a plain looking web page like this:

Hello, welcome to my website!

Watch this page grow as we use more and more components from Bootstrap!

Lorem ipsum dolor sit amet, consectetur adipiscing elit. Suspendisse consequat pretium diam, vitae mattis lorem dignissim a. Aenean rhoncus odio risus, non rhoncus diam posuere sed. Maecenas imperdiet velit sed lacus ornare, dictum feugiat tellus vestibulum. Sed semper ipsum et luctus pretium. Suspendisse ac dui eu quam sodales accumsan. Ut ultrices neque nisi, sagittis accumsan sapien fringilla non. Proin facilisis consequat euismod. Suspendisse a viverra elit, eget blandit tellus. Nam nec mollis tortor.

Curabitur a eros vitae nisi placerat luctus. Nullam viverra eleifend tincidunt. Lorem ipsum dolor sit amet, consectetur adipiscing elit. Phasellus interdum arcu a nunc sollicitudin, eu dignissim nisl tempor. Cras sit amet sollicitudin turpis. Quisque fringilla sem quis tellus eleifend mattis. Ut condimentum eros elit, et semper nunc tristique dignissim. Phasellus in mollis lorem. Donec porttitor tristique mollis. Aliquam quis arcu non elit mattis mollis at nec mi.

Sed non faucibus magna, et facilisis enim. Proin luctus commodo commodo. Aenean nulla leo, faucibus non consequat in, posuere quis tortor. Nam malesuada metus sit amet mi congue gravida. Vestibulum sit amet viverra metus. Etiam sit amet felis consequat, vulputate est nec, fermentum augue. Cras interdum sollicitudin libero ut tempus. Maecenas porttitor lacinia justo, eu placerat libero rutrum vel. Phasellus semper massa vel diam bibendum, sit amet convallis enim congue. Aliquam accumsan neque sit amet risus sodales vehicula. Curabitur vel mattis nisl, nec mattis dolor. In rutrum, leo at laoreet elementum, felis ipsum sagittis neque, in rutrum lacus nisl nec nulla.

Maecenas ac augue dignissim, tincidunt nibh quis, interdum odio. Curabitur tellus dolor, scelerisque vitae libero ac, fringilla vulputate augue. Cras vel convallis enim, non auctor ante. Suspendisse dapibus vel ligula at vehicula. Suspendisse nulla metus, molestie vel malesuada id, porttitor ut arcu. Proin et laoreet leo, blandit accumsan est. Curabitur sit amet nulla in dolor auctor pellentesque. Nullam id odio et nulla tincidunt imperdiet. Morbi ultrices lacinia diam, non porttitor sem dignissim eu. Maecenas et ultrices ipsum.

Figure 1.1

Into this:

Figure 1.2

Not only does the transformed page look better, it is also responsive. It rearranges itself nicely when viewed on a smaller display (Figure 1.3).

This book will demonstrate how to use Bootstrap's grid system to create a multi-column layout. It will also guide you in creating a navigation bar, different types of menus (with or without dropdowns), buttons, and icons. All this will be covered in Chapters 3 to 8.

Figure 1.3

Chapter 9 will cover forms and form validations. You will learn to create a simple Sign Up form with some validation procedures to examine the data entered and display a warning when appropriate.

Figure 1.4 gives you an example of a warning generated by the validation that you will be working on:

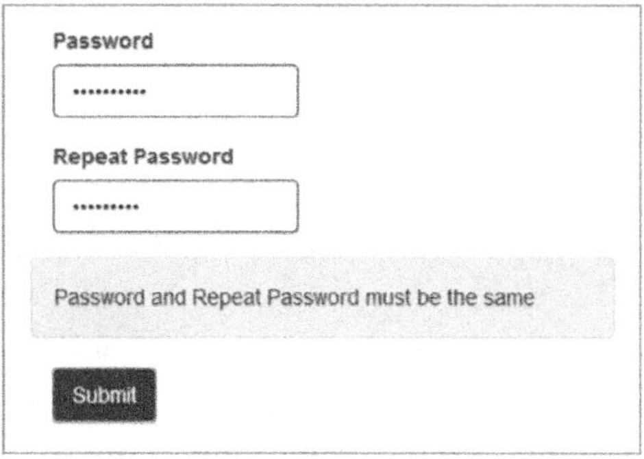

Password
Repeat Password
Password and Repeat Password must be the same
Submit

Figure 1.4

In Chapter 10, you will proceed to learn how to create a Modal window like the one below:

Login
User ID
Password
Cancel

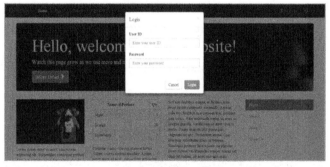

Figure 1.5

Chapter 11 will explain how to handle images and how to make them responsive.

Tables will be discussed in Chapter 12. This book will show you how to display tables and how to adjust the width of the tables and the columns.

Needless to say, this book will be incomplete

without a lesson on customizing Bootstrap to fit your own style. Chapter 13 covers light customization. It will illustrate how you can change fonts, colors and background images to make the page your own.

Light customization however is good only for minimal changes in the design. To tweak the design further, you will be better off using LESS. Chapter 14 is dedicated to this subject. You will learn how to work with LESS and how to customize it.

Towards the end of the book, we will throw in some more Bootstrap components that can increase your site's appeal. You will learn to create a carousel that looks like below:

Figure 1.6

You will also learn about Affix, Scrollspy, Tooltip, Popover, Collapse and Progress Bar. They are covered in Chapters 16 to 21. Not only you will know how to display them, you will also utilize some of the controls to make them work. A progress bar for example, would be pointless if it is displayed statically. We need to know how to control it to make it work as a progress bar.

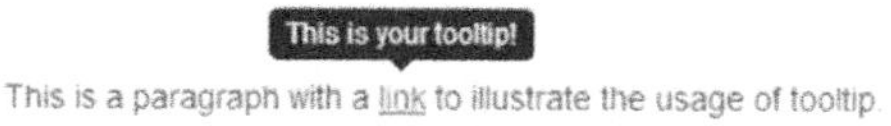

This is your tooltip!

This is a paragraph with a link to illustrate the usage of tooltip

Figure 1.7. Tooltip

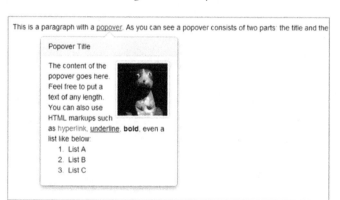

Figure 1.8. Popover

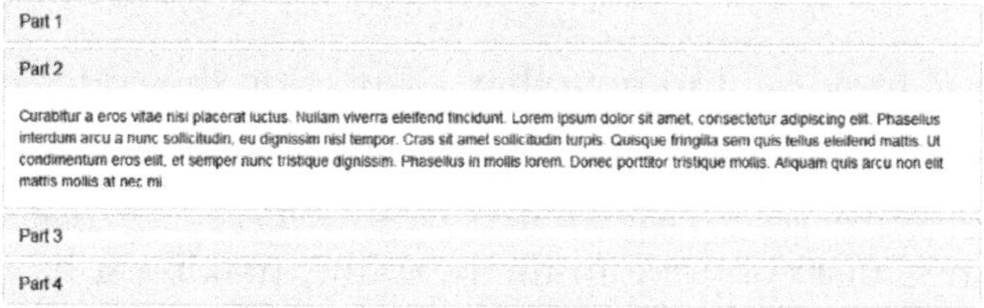

Figure 1.9. Collapse

Figure 1.10. Progress Bar

As the last lesson of the book, you will learn one of the most important features when creating a responsive page: How to show or hide certain parts of the page depending on the size of the screen. This will be covered in Chapter 22.

For absolute beginners, quick introductions to CSS, LESS and compiling LESS are provided in the appendices.

Conventions in this book

Since this is a programming book, there will be some codes involved. All codes will be displayed as follows:

```
The codes
will be displayed
this way
```

It is important to note that displaying the codes in a tiny paperback such as this can be challenging at times. A line of codes that is too long to fit in one line must continue to the next line, making it hard to know at a glance whether it is one line or two separate lines of codes.

In order to make it easier for you, whenever a line of code is broken into two or more lines, you will see this symbol:

↵

Whenever you see that symbol, you will know that the next line is just a continuation of the previous one. See the illustration below:

```
This is a one-liner

This text has only one line but its width ↵
exceeds the width of the page and has to ↵
continue to the next line.

This text has two lines. This is the first.
And this is the second.
```

If you find it difficult to read the codes in this book you can always download them using the links provided and view them on your computer.

In every lesson there will be a *View on Browser* link for you to view the examples. Just open it on a web browser and that particular example will be displayed. Please bear in mind that you will need to be connected to the internet or the examples will not work.

Depending on the type of device that you use, the result you see may be slightly different from the screenshots presented. (It is responsive to screen size, remember?) Just bear this in mind when you run the examples and stumble upon some inconsistencies.

You can also download the examples by following the Download link inside every chapter. They come in zipped files. To run the downloaded file simply unzip it into your computer and open it using a web browser. If you prefer to download all the examples in one zip file, the link will be provided at the end of the book (Page 194). All examples have been reviewed and tested to work prior to publication.

Are you ready to get started? Let's get to work!

2

GETTING STARTED

Let's start by creating an HTML page. This is going to be our working page and we will add more and more components into it as we go on.

Below is an example of a simple HTML page:

```
<!DOCTYPE html>
<html>

    <head>
        <meta charset="UTF-8">
        <title>Welcome</title>
    </head>

    <body>

        <h1>Hello, welcome to my website!</h1>

        <p>Watch this page grow as we use ↵
        More and more components ↵
        from Bootstrap!</p>

        <p>Paragraph 1…</p>
        <p>Paragraph 2…</p>
        <p>Paragraph 3…</p>
```

```
      <p>Paragraph 4...</p>
   </body>
```

```
</html>
```

Note:

Feel free to add more text to all the paragraphs to allow them to fill the page. In our example we will use page fillers.

The page will look like below:

Figure 2.1

View on browser: http://bit.ly/p-start
Download: http://bit.ly/dl-start

We will save this file as *index.html*. You are free to name it differently if you prefer.

Before we can implement Bootstrap in this HTML page, we need to get the necessary files. There are two ways:

1. Download Bootstrap

We can download all the necessary files from:

```
http://getbootstrap.com/getting-
started/#download/
```

Select the compiled and minified option. At the time of this book's publication, the latest version available is v3.2.0. This is the version that we will be using throughout this book.

Note:
For the moment, there is no need to download the source code or the Sass. However, later on when we are working on the LESS customization (chapter 14 page 120), we will need the source code.

When the downloaded file is unzipped, it produces three folders: *css*, *fonts* and *js*.

Create a new folder, for example `C:\bootstrap` (you can name the folder anything you want), and save the *css*, *fonts* and *js* folders there. This is our working folder, and we will be using this very same folder throughout all of our exercises.

In addition to the files above, Bootstrap requires JQuery to run. We therefore need to download it as well. You can obtain JQuery by visiting:

```
http://jquery.com/download
```

At the time of publication, the latest version is 1.11.1. Make sure you download the compressed production version of it:

```
http://code.jquery.com/jquery-1.11.1.min.js
```

Save it our working folder (in our case it is `c:\bootstrap`).

Now that we have all the necessary files, let's apply them to our page. Notice the highlighted parts:

```
<!DOCTYPE html>

<html>

    <head>
        <meta charset="UTF-8">
        <title>Welcome</title>
        <link href="bootstrap/css/
        bootstrap.min.css" rel="stylesheet">
    </head>

    <body>

        <h1>Hello, welcome to my website!</h1>

        <p>Watch this page grow as we use
        more and more components from
        Bootstrap!</p>

        <p>Paragraph 1</p>
        <p>Paragraph 2</p>
        <p>Paragraph 3</p>
        <p>Paragraph 4</p>

        <script src="bootstrap/
        jquery-1.11.1.min.js"></script>
```

```
        <script src="bootstrap/js/ ↵
        bootstrap.min.js"> </script>

    </body>
</html>
```

We will use this option when we are working on the LESS customization in Chapter 14 (page 120).

2. Using CDN

Another way of obtaining Bootstrap is by using its Content Delivery Network (CDN). There are some obvious benefits gained by doing this. There is no download to do and therefore no need to store the files anywhere. We simply link to them using the CDN links provided.

Furthermore, since Bootstrap is quite popular, there is a good chance that prior to your site, your visitors have visited other sites that also use Bootstrap's CDNs and their browsers have cached the files locally. When they arrive at your site, their browsers will just reuse the cached files. Efficient!

The links to the CDNs are as follows:

CSS:

```
http://maxcdn.bootstrapcdn.com/
bootstrap/3.2.0/css/bootstrap.min.css
```

JS:

```
http:// maxcdn.bootstrapcdn.com/
bootstrap/3.2.0/js/bootstrap.min.js
```

And since Bootstrap requires JQuery to run, we need its CDN as well:

```
http://code.jquery.com/jquery-1.11.1.min.js
```

Let's use them in our page:

```
<!DOCTYPE html>
<html>

    <head>
        <meta charset="UTF-8">

        <link href="http://maxcdn. ↵
        bootstrapcdn.com/bootstrap/3.2.0/ ↵
        css/bootstrap.min.css" ↵
        rel="stylesheet">

        <title>Welcome</title>

    </head>

    <body>

        <h1>Hello, welcome to my website!</h1>

        <p>Watch this page grow as we use ↵
        more and more components from ↵
        Bootstrap!</p>

        <p>Paragraph 1….</p>
        <p>Paragraph 2….</p>
```

```
<p>Paragraph 3... </p>
<p>Paragraph 4....</p>

<script src="http://code.jquery.com/ ↵
jquery-1.11.1.min.js"></script>

<script src="http://maxcdn. ↵
bootstrapcdn.com/bootstrap/3.2.0/ ↵
js/bootstrap.min.js"></script>

    </body>
</html>
...
```

Note:

From this point onwards, this book will use the CDNs in most of the examples. Having said that, to view the examples you will need to be connected to the internet or they will not work.

The only time we do not use the bootstrap.min.css from the CDN is when we are working on the LESS customization in Chapter 14 (page 120).

Before we take a look at how the changes we did in this chapter affect our HTML page, there is a little bit more to add:

```
<!DOCTYPE html>

<html>

    <head>

        <meta charset="UTF-8">
        <meta http-equiv="X-UA-Compatible" ↵
        content="IE=edge">
```

17

```
<meta name="viewport" ↵
content="width=device-width, ↵
initial-scale=1">
```
...

Explanation:

We added the following to our page:

1. **`<meta http-equiv="X-UA-Compatible" content="IE=edge">`**

   This is useful in case our page is opened using Internet Explorer. It basically tells the browser to render the page using the latest rendering engine.

2. **`<meta name="viewport" content="width=device-width, initial-scale=1">`**

   We need this to optimize our page to mobile devices. The `width = device-width` sets the width of the page to follow the screen-width of the device (which will vary depending on the device), and the `initial-scale = 1` sets the initial level of zoom when the page is first loaded by the browser.

Let's end this chapter by looking at how all the changes above affect our HTML page:

Figure 2.2

View on browser: http://bit.ly/p-cdn
Download: http://bit.ly/dl-cdn

Don't worry about the margin on the left and right. We will take care of that in a moment.

3

CONTAINER & CONTAINER-FLUID

We will use container a lot in our exercises. It sets the width and paddings of the content that we put inside it. Let's try it:

```
...
<body>
    <div class="container">
        <h1>Hello, welcome to my website!</h1>
        <p>Watch this page grow as we use ↵
        more and more components from ↵
        Bootstrap!</p>
    </div>

    <div class="container">
        <p>Paragraph 1</p>
        <p>Paragraph 2</p>
        <p>Paragraph 3</p>
        <p>Paragraph 4</p>
    </div>
...
```

Our page now looks like below:

Figure 3.1

View on browser: http://bit.ly/p-cntr
Download: http://bit.ly/dl-cntr

We can use more than one container in a page, as long as it is not one inside the other.

We can do this:

```
<div class="container">
    Some content here
</div>

<div class="container">
    Some more content here
</div>
```

But not this:

```
<div class="container">
    Some content here
    <div class="container">
        Some more content here
    </div>
</div>
```

If we would like our page to fill the whole screen, we can change the `<div class="container">` to `<div class="container-fluid">`.

21

Our page will become:

Figure 3.2

Note:

When viewed on mobile devices, the difference between container and container-fluid may not be noticeable.

View on browser: http://bit.ly/p-cntrf
Download: http://bit.ly/dl-cntrf

4

JUMBOTRON

Right now the greeting *"Hello, welcome to my website!"* and the text below it blend too much with the rest of the content. Let's make them more prominent by placing them inside a Jumbotron.

See below:

```
...
...
<body>

<div class="container">
    <div class="jumbotron">
        <h1>Hello, welcome to my website!</h1>
        <p>Watch this page grow as we use ↵
        More and more components ↵
        from Bootstrap!</p>
    </div>
</div>

<div class="container">
    <p>Paragraph 1...</p>
    <p>Paragraph 2...</p>
    <p>Paragraph 3...</p>
```

```
    <p>Paragraph 4...</p>
</div>
...
...
```

Our page now looks like this:

Figure 4.1

View on browser: http://bit.ly/p-jmb
Download: http://bit.ly/dl-jmb

Explanation:

Jumbotron enlarges the font sizes of both the header `<h1>` and the paragraph `<p>`, and puts them in a box with rounded corners and gray background color.

What if we want to use different colors for the background and the text inside the Jumbotron? Can we do that? Yes, of course. It will be covered later in the chapter on light customization (Page 111).

5

BUTTONS

Bootstrap provides some styled buttons right out of the box. To use a button simply write:

```
class="btn btn-default"
```

We can use it in the HTML tag for buttons:

```
<button type="button" class="btn ↵
btn-default">Button Name</button>
```

or in a link:

```
<a href="..." class="btn btn-default"> ↵
Button Name</a>
```

It will create a button like this:

Button Name

Other than the `btn-default` that we used above,

Bootstrap also gives us `btn-primary`, `btn-success`, `btn-info`, `btn-warning`, `btn-danger` and `btn-link`, all with their own background colors. `btn-success`, for example, is green, `btn-warning` is orange and `btn-danger` is red.

We can create buttons in various sizes as well:

Large: `btn-lg`

Small: `btn-sm`

Extra small: `btn-xs`

Note:
For more details see
http://getbootstrap.com/css/#buttons

Let's try to put a button in our Jumbotron. We will use `btn-primary` and set the size to large (`btn-lg`):

```
...
...
<div class="container">
    <div class="jumbotron">
        <h1>Hello, welcome to my website!</h1>
        <p>Watch this page grow as we use ↵
        more and more components from ↵
        Bootstrap!</p>
        <a href="#" class="btn ↵
        btn-primary btn-lg"> More Detail</a>
    </div>
</div>
...
...
```

Note:

Since we don't have any page to link it to, we put # as the link. In real life the "More Detail" page should be created so the button can link to it.

Let's see how it looks:

Figure 5.1

View on browser: http://bit.ly/p-btn
Download: http://bit.ly/dl-btn

6

ICONS

Bootstrap has 200 icons we can use for free. Since they are provided by *Glyphicons.com*, icons are referred to as glyphicons in Bootstrap. For the full list of available glyphicons, go to:

```
http://getbootstrap.com/components/
#glyphicons
```

Below is an example of how to display an icon:

```
<span class="glyphicon glyphicon-search> ↵
                </span>
```

In the example above we pick a *Search* glyphicon, which will display this:

Q

Let's try to put an icon on our new button. We will

put a right-chevron icon after the *"More Detail"* label. The name for this icon is **glyphicon-chevron-right**.

```
...
<div class="container">
    <div class="jumbotron">
        <h1>Hello, welcome to my website!</h1>
        <p>Watch this page grow as we use ↵
        more and more components from ↵
        Bootstrap!</p>

        <a href="#" class="btn ↵
        btn-primary btn-lg">More Detail ↵
        <span class="glyphicon ↵
        glyphicon-chevron-right"></span> ↵
        </a>
    </div>
</div>
...
```

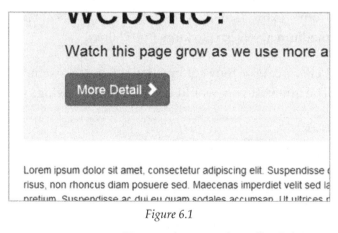

Figure 6.1

View on browser: http://bit.ly/p-icon
Download: http://bit.ly/dl-icon

7

MULTI-COLUMN LAYOUT

With Bootstrap we can easily create a multi-column layout that can scale up to 12 columns. These columns will rearrange themselves when viewed on different screen sizes. By default they are designed to cater to screens with sizes ranging from extra small (<768px), small (>=768px), medium (>=992px) to large (>=1200px).

Let's create a four-column layout as an example. The quickest way would be to do the following:

```
...
<div class="container">
    <div class="row">
        <div class="col-md-3">Column 1</div>
        <div class="col-md-3">Column 2</div>
        <div class="col-md-3">Column 3</div>
        <div class="col-md-3">Column 4</div>
    </div>
</div>
...
```

Explanation:

We start with a container. Inside it we create a row by using `<div class="row">...</div>`. Inside this row we put our columns by using `<div class="col-md-3">...</div>`.

The `col-md-3` can be translated as follows: `col` means column. `md` is the screen size that we are targeting, in this case it is the medium-sized screen. Other notations for sizes would be `xs` for extra small, `sm` for small, and `lg` for large.

The number 3 indicates the size of the column. Remember we mentioned previously that Bootstrap by default can scale up to 12 columns? This means if we want to create a 12-column layout of equal width, we would write `<div class="col-md-1"> ... </div>` twelve times.

If we want to create a 6-column layout, we would write `<div class="col-md-2">...</div>` six times.

Therefore, to create a 4-column layout, we put `<div class="col-md-3">...</div>` four times, as you can see in the example above.

Let's change our page's layout to four-columns. Feel free to add more text if you need to fill the space.

```
...
<div class="container">
    <div class="row">
        <div class="col-md-3">
            <p>Paragraph 1</p>
        </div>
        <div class="col-md-3">
            <p>Paragraph 2</p>
        </div>
        <div class="col-md-3">
            <p>Paragraph 3</p>
        </div>
        <div class="col-md-3">
            <p>Paragraph 4</p>
        </div>
    </div>
</div>
...
```

On a large screen the page will look like below:

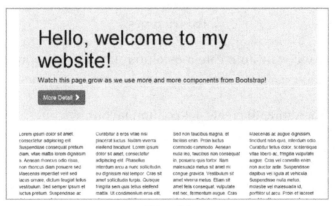

Figure 7.1

View on browser: http://bit.ly/p-mcol
Download: http://bit.ly/dl-mcol

Note:

Certain types of browsers on mobile devices would fall into a small screen category, and therefore may not display the page as shown in the screenshot above.

How would our page look when viewed on a small screen?

Our page has automatically adjusted itself into a single-column layout. With Bootstrap, the page is now responsive to the size of the screen and adjusts itself accordingly.

Figure 7.2

Note:

If you are working on a computer and would like to see how the page looks on a mobile device, you do not need to actually use a tablet or a phone. Just open the page using modern browsers such as Mozilla Firefox or Google Chrome, and resize the window by shrinking or expanding it to see how the page behaves on various screen sizes. This is quicker than switching back and forth between a computer and a tablet or a phone.

So far we have been working on creating multiple columns of equal width. What if we want them to be of different widths? In order to do that, we will need to play with the numbers.

For example, if we want to create a three-column layout where the first column is wider than the second column and the second is wider than the third, we can do the following:

```
...
<div class="container">
    <div class="row">
        <div class="col-md-6">Column 1</div>
        <div class="col-md-4">Column 2</div>
        <div class="col-md-2">Column 3</div>
    </div>
</div>
...
```

Let's go further: Up to now our page has been displayed either as a four-column or a single-column layout depending on the screen size. How about creating a little transition: On a large screen, display as four-columns. On a medium screen, two-columns. On a small screen, a single-column.

How do we do that? Remember the notation xs, sm, md and lg for the screen sizes? In the above example we have only used md, which means we only cater for medium-sized screens.

Now let's write for all screen sizes:

```
<div class="col-xs-12 col-sm-12 col-md-6 ↵
col-lg-3">...</div>
```

Explanation:

`col-xs-12` `col-sm-12` can be read as: "When displayed on extra small (`xs`) and small (`sm`) screens, display in one column."

`col-md-6`: "On medium (`md`) sized screens, display in two columns."

`col-lg-3`: "On large (`lg`) screens, four columns."

Let's update our page:

```
...
<div class="container">
    <div class="row">
        <div class="col-xs-12 col-sm-12 ↵
        col-md-6 col-lg-3">
            <p>Paragraph 1...</p>
        </div>
        <div class="col-xs-12 col-sm-12 ↵
        col-md-6 col-lg-3">
            <p>Paragraph 2...</p>
        </div>
        <div class="col-xs-12 col-sm-12 ↵
        col-md-6 col-lg-3">
            <p>Paragraph 3...</p>
        </div>
        <div class="col-xs-12 col-sm-12 ↵
        col-md-6 col-lg-3">
            <p>Paragraph 4...</p>
        </div>
    </div>
</div>
...
```

When viewed on a large screen, our page looks like this:

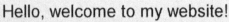

Figure 7.3

On a medium screen:

Figure 7.4

It turns into a two-column layout. (However, something is not right. Paragraph 3 should be in the first column, right below Paragraph 1. Paragraph 4 should be at the same level as Paragraph 3 and not below it. Don't worry. We will explain how to fix this problem in a moment.)

On a small screen:

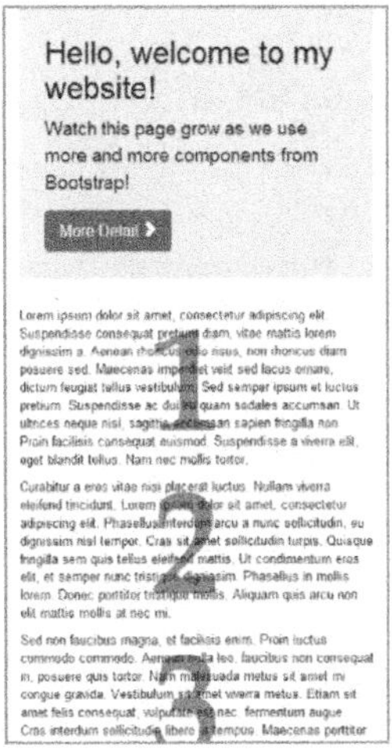

Figure 7.5

As you can see, depending on the screen size, our page will display the number of columns exactly the way we want it to.

View on browser:
http://bit.ly/p-mcol2

Download:
http://bit.ly/dl-mcol2

Now let's fix the problem that we have when the page is displayed as a two-column layout. Sometimes when the columns vary in height, they do not rearrange as expected. In our case, the first paragraph is taller than the second. This creates some empty space below the second paragraph, and the third paragraph goes there to fill it instead of going to the first column below the first paragraph.

See the illustration below. The dark gray boxes indicate the height of the respective paragraphs.

See how the first paragraph is a little bit taller than the second.

Figure 7.6

If we would like the first and second paragraph to have the same height regardless of content, we can use what Bootstrap calls a column reset. It will set the height of the whole row based on the height of the tallest member in that row. In our case, the height of the first row will follow the height of the first paragraph.

To use column reset we write:

```
<div class="clearfix visible-**"></div>
```

Replace ** with the screen size that we have a

problem with. In the case above, we have a problem with the medium-sized screen, therefore:

```
<div class="clearfix visible-md"></div>
```

Where do we place it? Since the problem occurred when the page is displayed as a two-column layout, we place it right after the second column.

To be safe, just in case the same problem arises when the page is displayed as a four-column layout, we also put:

```
<div class="clearfix visible-lg"></div>
```

and we place it right after the fourth column.

```
...
<div class="container">
    <div class="row">
        <div class="col-xs-12 col-sm-12 ↵
        col-md-6 col-lg-3">
            <p>Paragraph 1...</p>
        </div>
        <div class="col-xs-12 col-sm-12 ↵
        col-md-6 col-lg-3">
            <p>Paragraph 2...</p>
        </div>
        <div class="clearfix ↵
        visible-md"></div>
        <div class="col-xs-12 col-sm-12 ↵
        col-md-6 col-lg-3">
            <p>Paragraph 3...</p>
        </div>
        <div class="col-xs-12 col-sm-12 ↵
        col-md-6 col-lg-3">
            <p>Paragraph 4.</p>
        </div>
```

```
    <div class="clearfix ↵
    visible-lg"></div>
  </div>
</div>
...
```

Let's display our page again on a medium-sized screen:

Figure 7.7

The problem is solved!

View on browser: http://bit.ly/p-mcol3
Download: http://bit.ly/dl-mcol3

8

WORKING WITH NAVIGATION

Our website will eventually contain more than one page and we need to provide our visitors with a way to navigate around the site. In this chapter we will explore some of what Bootstrap has to offer when it comes to creating navigation menus.

First let's create our menu. Since we only have one page so far, we will make something up. We will create three menu-items called *Menu 1* to *3*.

```
<ul>
    <li><a href="#">Home</a></li>
    <li><a href="#">Menu 1</a></li>
    <li><a href="#">Menu 2</a></li>
    <li><a href="#">Menu 3</a></li>
</ul>
```

Note:
Since we don't have the pages to link the menu items to, we put "#" as the links. This way when the menu items are clicked, we will not get the "page not found" message.

We have two options for how we can display this menu: Tabs or Pills. Let's see which one we prefer.

8.1 Tabs

We create Tabs by using the class `nav nav-tabs`:

```
<ul class="nav nav-tabs">
    <li><a href="#">Home</a></li>
    <li><a href="#">Menu 1</a></li>
    <li><a href="#">Menu 2</a></li>
    <li><a href="#">Menu 3</a></li>
</ul>
```

Let's use it in our page. We will place our menu below the Jumbotron.

```
...
<div class="container">
    <div class="jumbotron">
        <h1>Hello, welcome to my website!</h1>
        <p>Watch this page grow as we use ↵
        more and more components from ↵
        Bootstrap!</p>
        <a href="#" class="btn btn-primary ↵
        btn-lg">More Detail <span class= ↵
        "glyphicon glyphicon-chevron-right"> ↵
        </span></a>
    </div>
</div>

<div class="container">
    <ul class="nav nav-tabs">
        <li><a href="#">Home</a></li>
        <li><a href="#">Menu 1</a></li>
        <li><a href="#">Menu 2</a></li>
        <li><a href="#">Menu 3</a></li>
    </ul>
</div>
```

```
<div class="container">
    <div class="row">
        <div class="col-xs-12 col-sm-12 col- ↵
        md-6 col-lg-3">
            <p>Paragraph 1</p>
        </div>
...
```

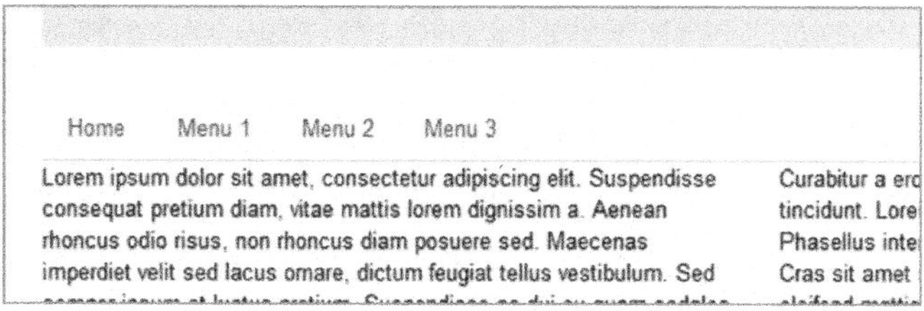

Figure 8.1

View on browser: http://bit.ly/p-tab
Download: http://bit.ly/dl-tab

You may think that they don't look much like Tabs at this point. It is because we are missing one thing: Our page is the *Home* page. We therefore should mark the menu item *Home* as active.

```
...
<div class="container">
    <ul class="nav nav-tabs">
        <li class="active"><a href="#"> ↵
        Home</a></li>
        <li><a href="#">Menu 1</a></li>
        <li><a href="#">Menu 2</a></li>
        <li><a href="#">Menu 3</a></li>
    </ul>
</div>
...
```

See the difference:

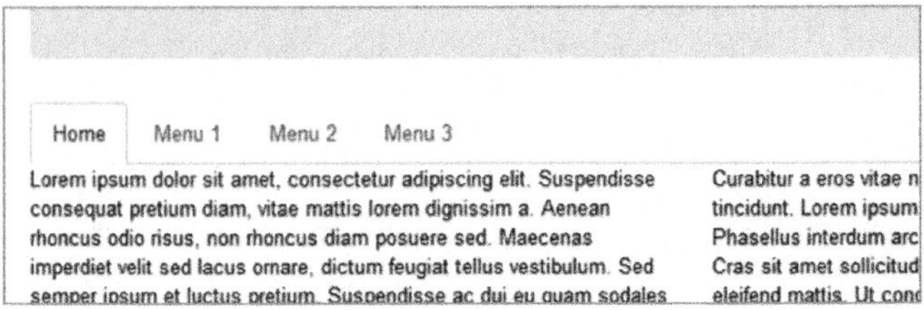

Figure 8.2

View on browser: http://bit.ly/p-tab2
Download: http://bit.ly/dl-tab2

Note:
You must have noticed that the four-column texts are placed awfully close to our Tabs. That does not look very nice, does it? We will address this in Chapter 13 (Page 111). For now, let's focus on the Menu.

It is important to note that the menu arrangement above has its limitations. If we put more menu items than what can fit in one line, the layout does not look as good. See below:

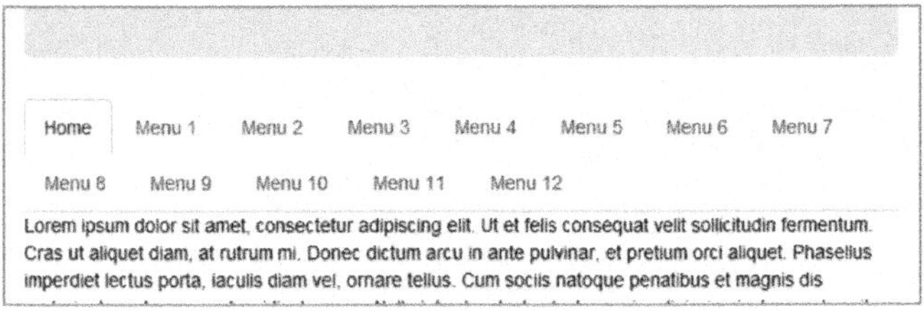

Figure 8.3

8.2 Pills

To use Pills we write:

```
class="nav nav-pills"
```

Let's give it a try:

```
...
<div class="container">
    <ul class="nav nav-pills">
        <li class="active">
            <a href="#">Home</a>
        </li>
        <li><a href="#">Menu 1</a></li>
        <li><a href="#">Menu 2</a></li>
        <li><a href="#">Menu 3</a></li>
    </ul>
</div>
...
```

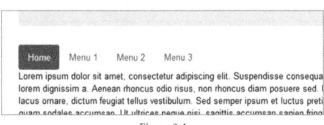

Figure 8.4

View on browser: http://bit.ly/p-pills
Download: http://bit.ly/dl-pills

We can also display the Pills vertically:

```
class="nav nav-pills nav-stacked"
```

45

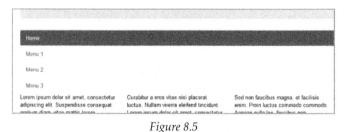

Figure 8.5

View on browser: http://bit.ly/p-pills2
Download: http://bit.ly/dl-pills2

On second thought, under the Jumbotron may not be the best place to put the vertical menu. Let's place it inside one of the columns instead.

In our page we have four paragraphs that make up the four columns. Replace the last paragraph with the Pills that we have.

```
...
<div class="container">
    <div class="row">
        <div class="col-xs-12 col-sm-12 ↵
        col-md-6 col-lg-3">
            <p>Paragraph 1...</p>
        </div>

        <div class="col-xs-12 col-sm-12 ↵
        col-md-6 col-lg-3">
            <p>Paragràph 2...</p>
        </div>

        <div class="clearfix ↵
        visible-md"></div>

        <div class="col-xs-12 col-sm-12 ↵
        col-md-6 col-lg-3">
```

```
    <p>Paragraph 3...</p>

</div>

<div class="col-xs-12 col-sm-12 ↵
col-md-6 col-lg-3">

    <ul class="nav nav-pills ↵
    nav-stacked">
        <li class="active">
        <a href="#">Home</a>
        </li>
        <li><a href="#">Menu 1</a> ↵
        </li>
        <li><a href="#">Menu 2</a> ↵
        </li>
        <li><a href="#">Menu 3</a> ↵
        </li>
    </ul>

</div>

<div class="clearfix visible-lg"> ↵
</div>

</div>
</div>
...
```

Figure 8.6

View on browser: http://bit.ly/p-pills3
Download: http://bit.ly/dl-pills3

Note:

When viewed on a small screen, because the page rearranges itself into one column, the menu automatically moves to the bottom.

8.3 Dropdown Menu

Let's go back to our Tabs page and see how we can add a dropdown to one of the menu items. As an example, we will add a dropdown menu to *Menu 3*.

Below is what we have for our Tabs so far:

```
...
<div class="container">
    <ul class="nav nav-tabs">
        <li class="active">
            <a href="#">Home</a>
        </li>
        <li><a href="#">Menu 1</a></li>
        <li><a href="#">Menu 2</a></li>
        <li><a href="#">Menu 3</a></li>
    </ul>
</div>
...
```

Let's add some submenu items to *Menu 3*:

```
...
<div class="container">
    <ul class="nav nav-tabs">
        <li class="active">
            <a href="#">Home</a>
        </li>
        <li><a href="#">Menu 1</a></li>
        <li><a href="#">Menu 2</a></li>

        <li class="dropdown">
```

```
<a class="dropdown-toggle"
data-toggle="dropdown"
href="#">Menu 3 <span
class="caret"></span></a>
<ul class="dropdown-menu">
    <li>
        <a href="#">Submenu
        3 - 1</a>
    </li>
    <li>
        <a href="#">Submenu
        3 - 2</a>
    </li>
    <li>
        <a href="#">Submenu
        3 - 3</a>
    </li>
    <li>
        <a href="#">Submenu
        3 - 4</a>
    </li>
    </ul>
</li>
    </ul>
</div>
...
```

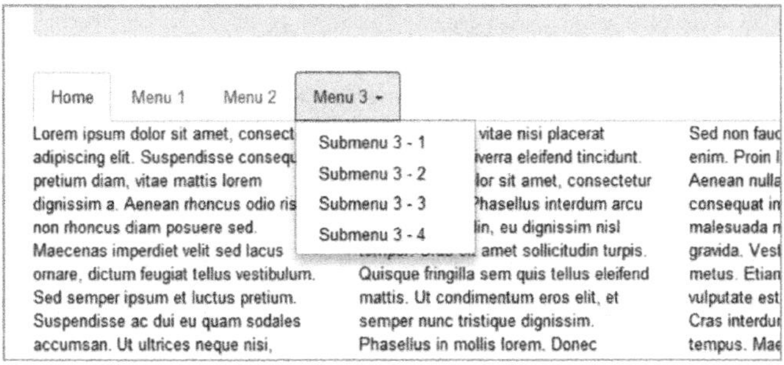

Figure 8.7

View on browser: http://bit.ly/p-tabdrop
Download: http://bit.ly/dl-tabdrop

Can we do the same with the Pills? Of course.
Remember we have placed our Pills on the fourth
column:

```
...
<div class="col-xs-12 col-sm-12 col-md-6 ↵
col-lg-3">
    <p>Paragraph 3...</p>
</div>

<div class="col-xs-12 col-sm-12 col-md-6 ↵
col-lg-3">

    <ul class="nav nav-pills nav-stacked">
        <li class="active">
            <a href="#">Home</a>
        </li>
        <li><a href="#">Menu 1</a></li>
        <li><a href="#">Menu 2</a></li>

        <li class="dropdown">
            <a class="dropdown-toggle" ↵
            data-toggle="dropdown" ↵
            href="#">Menu 3 <span ↵
            class="caret"></span></a>
            <ul class="dropdown-menu">
                <li>
                    <a href="#">Submenu ↵
                    3 - 1</a>
                </li>
                <li>
                    <a href="#">Submenu ↵
                    3 - 2</a>
                </li>
                <li>
                    <a href="#">Submenu ↵
                    3 - 3</a>
                </li>
                <li>
                    <a href="#">Submenu ↵
                    3 - 4</a>
                </li>
```

```
        </ul>
       </li>
     </ul>
   </div>
<div class="clearfix visible-lg"></div>
...
```

See the result below:

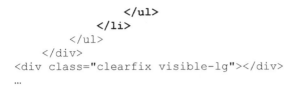

Figure 8.8

View on browser: http://bit.ly/p-pilldrop
Download: http://bit.ly/dl-pilldrop

8.4 Navigation Bar

Navigation Bar, or NavBar in Bootstrap terms, is a navigation header. It is placed at the top of the screen and can extend or collapse in accordance with the screen size.

This is how a navigation bar looks:

Figure 8.9

The navigation bar is at the top of the page and in this example it consists of the website's name (We call it *MyWebsite*), and four buttons: *Home*, *Page A*, *Page B* and *Page C*.

Note:
It may be a little redundant to have a Home button in the navigation bar when we already have the same button on our menu. The reason we put it in the navigation bar is to show how the button will look when it is set to active.

Below you can find the codes to create that navigation bar:

```
...
<body>

    <nav class="navbar navbar-default">

        <div class="container-fluid">
            <div class="navbar-header">
                <a class="navbar-brand" ↵
                href="#">MyWebsite</a>
            </div>

            <div>
                <ul class="nav navbar-nav">
                    <li class="active">
                        <a href="#">Home</a>
```

```
                    </li>
                    <li>
                        <a href="#">Page A</a>
                    </li>
                    <li>
                        <a href="#">Page B</a>
                    </li>
                    <li>
                        <a href="#">Page C</a>
                    </li>
                </ul>
            </div>

        </div>

    </nav>

    <div class="container">

        <div class="jumbotron">

            <h1>Hello, welcome to my ↵
            website!</h1>
            <p>Watch this page grow as ↵
            we use more and more components ↵
            from Bootstrap!</p>
            <a href="#" class="btn ↵
            btn-primary btn-lg">More Detail ↵
            <span class="glyphicon glyphicon-↵
            chevron-right"></span></a>
        </div>

    </div>
...
```

View on browser: http://bit.ly/p-navbar
Download: http://bit.ly/dl-navbar

Note:
If you are viewing the page on a browser using a mobile device, the navigation bar may not appear like the

screenshot above. We will discuss displaying the navigation bar on small screens a little later.

8.4.1 Inverted Navigation Bar

If we don't like the style of the default navigation bar, Bootstrap provides an alternative. It is the inverted version of the default. To use it, change the `navbar-default` into `navbar-inverse`.

```
...
<nav class="navbar navbar-inverse">

    <div class="container-fluid">

        <div class="navbar-header">
            <a class="navbar-brand" ↵
            href="#">MyWebsite</a>
        </div>
...
```

Figure 8.10

View on browser: http://bit.ly/p-navinv
Download: http://bit.ly/dl-navinv

We will keep this version for our exercise.

8.4.2 Fixed Navigation Bar

So far the navigation bar that we created has been static: It moves with the page as we scroll. Another option is to have it fixed, where the navigation bar stays visible in a fixed position independent of the page scrolls.

This is a good option to go for if we have a lengthy page and users are likely to scroll down. Having the navigation bar visible at all times gives the users access to it without having to scroll back all the way up.

Let's try it. We will have the navigation bar fixed at the top of the page. (Feel free to add more text if the current one is not long enough to allow the page to scroll.)

```
...
<nav class="navbar navbar-inverse navbar- ↵
fixed-top">

    <div class="container-fluid">
        <div class="navbar-header">
            <a class="navbar-brand" ↵
            href="#">MyWebsite</a>
        </div>

        <div>
            <ul class="nav navbar-nav">
                <li class="active">
                    <a href="#"> Home</a>
                </li>
                <li>
                    <a href="#">Page A</a>
```

```
                    </li>
                    <li>
                         <a href="#">Page B</a>
                    </li>
                    <li>
                         <a href="#">Page C</a>
                    </li>
               </ul>
           </div>
       </div>

</nav>
...
```

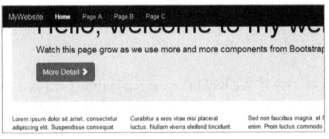

Figure 8.11

View on browser: http://bit.ly/p-navfix
Download: http://bit.ly/dl-navfix

Try to scroll down and see how the navigation bar stays on the screen.

If we can have the navigation bar fixed at the top, can we have it fixed at the bottom? Yes. Just change the `navbar-fixed-top` to `navbar-fixed-bottom` and our navigation bar will be fixed at the bottom.

```
...
<nav class="navbar navbar-inverse ↵
navbar-fixed-bottom">
```

```
<div class="container-fluid">

    <div class="navbar-header">
        <a class="navbar-brand" ↵
        href="#">MyWebsite</a>
    </div>
...
```

Figure 8.12

View on browser: http://bit.ly/p-navfixb
Download: http://bit.ly/dl-navfixb

8.4.3 Navigation Bar with a Dropdown Menu

Just like with the Tabs and Pills, we can add a dropdown menu to the navigation bar. Let's try by adding a dropdown to the *Page C* button.

```
...
<nav class="navbar navbar-inverse">

    <div class="container-fluid">

        <div class="navbar-header">
            <a class="navbar-brand" ↵
            href="#">MyWebsite</a>
        </div>

        <div>
```

```html
<ul class="nav navbar-nav">
    <li class="active">
        <a href="#">Home</a>
    </li>
    <li><a href="#">Page A</a></li>
    <li><a href="#">Page B</a></li>

    <li class="dropdown">
        <a href="#" class="dropdown-
        toggle" data toggle=
        "dropdown">Page C <b
        class="caret"></b></a>
        <ul class="dropdown-menu">
            <li>
                <a href="#">Page C
                - 1</a>
            </li>
            <li>
                <a href="#">Page C
                - 2</a>
            </li>
            <li>
                <a href="#">Page C
                3</a>
            </li>
        </ul>
    </li>
</ul>

</div>
</div>
</nav>
...
```

If you remember, what we have done here is similar to what we did when we created a dropdown menu in 8.3.

See the result below:

Figure 8.13

View on browser: http://bit.ly/p-navdrop
Download: http://bit.ly/dl-navdrop

8.4.4 Right-Aligned Navigation Bar

Up to now all our navigation bar buttons have been
aligned to the left. What if in addition to that we
would like to have some buttons aligned to the
right? As an exercise we will create a *Login* and a
Sign Up button and we will align these buttons to
the right.

```
...
<nav class="navbar navbar-inverse">
    <div class="container-fluid">
        <div class="navbar-header">
            <a class="navbar-brand" ↵
            href="#">MyWebsite</a>
        </div>
        <div>
            <ul class="nav navbar-nav">
                <li class="active">
                    <a href="#">Home</a>
                </li>
                <li>
                    <a href="#">Page A</a>
                </li>
                <li>
                    <a href="#">Page B</a>
```

```
            </li>
            <li class="dropdown">
                <a href="#" class=" ↵
                dropdown-toggle" ↵
                data-toggle="dropdown"> ↵
                Page C <b class="caret"> ↵
                </b></a>
                <ul class="dropdown-menu">
                    <li><a href="#">Page C ↵
                    - 1</a></li>
                    <li><a href="#">Page C ↵
                    - 2</a></li>
                    <li><a href="#">Page C ↵
                    - 3</a></li>
                </ul>
            </li>
        </ul>

        <ul class="nav navbar-nav ↵
        navbar-right">
            <li>
                <a href="#">Sign Up</a>
            </li>
            <li>
                <a href="#">Login</a>
            </li>
        </ul>

    </div>
  </div>
</nav>
...
```

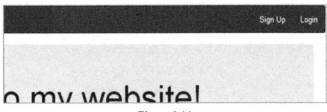

Figure 8.14

View on browser: http://bit.ly/p-navright
Download: http://bit.ly/dl-navright

Since we have learned how to use icons, let's add icons to these buttons. We will use *glyphicon-user* and *glyphicon-log-in*.

```
...
<ul class="nav navbar-nav navbar-right">
    <li>
        <a href="#"><span class="glyphicon ↵
        glyphicon-user"></span> Sign Up</a>
    </li>
    <li>
        <a href="#"><span class="glyphicon ↵
        glyphicon-log-in"></span> Login</a>
    </li>
</ul>
...
```

Figure 8.15

View on browser: http://bit.ly/p-navricon
Download: http://bit.ly/dl-navricon

8.4.5 Collapsing the Navigation Bar

We are quite happy with our navigation bar so far. That is until we view it on a small screen:

Figure 8.16

The navigation bar occupies a large part of the screen and is grabbing the attention away from the content. It would be better if we can hide the navigation bar and only show it when it is needed.

Something like below:

The navigation bar is hidden, replaced by this button on the top right corner:

The bar will only be displayed when we click the button.

Figure 8.17

How do we do this? See the part marked in boldface below:

```
...
<nav class="navbar navbar-inverse">
    <div class="container-fluid">
        <div class="navbar-header">
            <button type="button" class=
            "navbar-toggle" data-toggle=
            "collapse" data-target=
            "#myNavbar">
                <span class="icon-bar"></span>
                <span class="icon-bar"></span>
                <span class="icon-bar"></span>
            </button>
            <a class="navbar-brand"
            href="#">MyWebsite</a>

        </div>

        <div class="collapse navbar-collapse"
        id="myNavbar">

            <ul class="nav navbar-nav">
                <li class="active">
                    <a href="#">Home</a>
                </li>
                <li>
                    <a href="#">Page A</a>
                </li>
                <li>
                    <a href="#">Page B</a>
                </li>
                <li class="dropdown">
                    <a href="#" class=
                    "dropdown-toggle" data-
                    toggle="dropdown">Page C
                    <b class="caret"></b></a>
                    <ul class="dropdown-menu">
                        <li><a href="#">Page
                        C - 1</a></li>
                        <li><a href="#">Page
                        C - 2</a></li>
                        <li><a href="#">Page
                        C - 3</a></li>
                    </ul>
```

```
            </li>
        </ul>

        <ul class="nav navbar-nav ↵
        navbar-right">
            <li><a href="#"><span ↵
            class="glyphicon ↵
            glyphicon-user"></span> ↵
            Sign Up</a></li>
            <li><a href="#"><span ↵
            class="glyphicon ↵
            glyphicon-log-in"></span> ↵
            Login</a></li>
        </ul>

    </div>
    </div>
</nav>
...
```

Explanation:

We want to collapse our navigation bar and replace it with one button, so we need to create the button:

```
<button type="button" class="navbar-toggle"
data-toggle="collapse" data-
target="#myNavbar">
    <span class="icon-bar"></span>
    <span class="icon-bar"></span>
    <span class="icon-bar"></span>
</button>
```

We put three small vertical bars inside the button, as indicated by: <span class="icon-bar"> </span>. This will create the following button:

`data-target="#myNavbar"` indicates the ID of the part that will be affected when the button is clicked. That part is the navigation bar. Therefore we give the navigation bar the ID *myNavbar*. In addition to that, we use the class `collapse navbar-collapse` to make it collapsible.

```
...
<div class="collapse navbar-collapse" ↵
id="myNavbar">

<ul class="nav navbar-nav">
    <li class="active">
        <a href="#">Home</a>
    </li>
    <li>
        <a href="#">Page A</a>
    </li>
...
```

View on browser: http://bit.ly/p-navcol
Download: http://bit.ly/dl-navcol

Note:

On certain tablet sizes, viewing how the navigation bar extends and collapses can be as easy as turning the device's position from portrait to landscape or vice versa.

9

FORMS

In this chapter we will work with forms by creating a Sign Up page. This page will be linked to the Sign Up button that we created in 8.4.4. (Page 59)

The code for the Sign Up form is as follows:

```
<div class="container">
    <h1>Sign Up</h1>
    <form action="#" method="post">
        <div class="form-group">
            <label for="inputName"> ↵
            Name</label>
            <input type="text" class= ↵
            "form-control" id="inputName" ↵
            placeholder="Enter your name">
        </div>
        <div class="form-group">
            <label for="inputEmail">Email ↵
            Address</label>
            <input type="email" class= ↵
            "form-control" id="inputEmail" ↵
            placeholder="Enter your email ↵
            address">
        </div>
```

```
<div class="form-group">
    <label for="inputPassword"> ↵
    Password</label>
    <input type="password" class= ↵
    "form-control" id="inputPassword" >
</div>
<div class="form-group">
    <label for="inputRepeatPassword"> ↵
    Repeat Password</label>
    <input type="password" class= ↵
    "form-control" id= ↵
    "inputRepeatPassword">
</div>
<p><button type="submit" class="btn ↵
btn-primary">Submit</button></p>
</form>
</div>
```

Explanation:

We wrap the content of our Sign Up page inside the Container. The form itself is created by using the `<form>...</form>` tag.

```
<div class="container">

    <h1>Sign Up</h1>
    <form action="#" method="post">
...
    </form>

</div>
```

The `action=...` indicates the page it should go to when the submit button is clicked. Since we do not have the page to process the form, we put # in it.

The `method=...` determines the form's submission method. Here we use the POST method.

Note:
Other than POST, there is also GET. POST is used to request the web server to receive the data sent in the HTTP message body. GET is used to retrieve data from the web server.

We are creating four fields for our form: *Name*, *Email Address*, *Password* and *Repeat Password*. We are placing each field inside the `<div class="form-group">...</div>`, and in it we will put the respective labels and inputs.

For example, for the Name field, we write:

```
<div class="form-group">
    <label for="inputName">Name</label>
    <input type="text" class="form-control" ↵
    id="inputName" placeholder="Enter your ↵
    name">
</div>
```

On the label we indicate which field that particular label is intended for. In the above, the label *Name* is intended for *inputName*, which is the ID for the *Name* field.

The input type indicates various value types that we are using in this form (text, email and password). Placeholder is used to display a short hint inside a field. You don't have to use

Placeholder if you prefer not to. As can be seen above, we do not use Placeholders in our *Password* and *Repeat Password* fields.

Now let's put this form into a page. We will save this page as *signup.html*.

```
<!DOCTYPE html>
<html>

<head>
    <meta charset="UTF-8">
    <meta http-equiv="X-UA-Compatible"
    content="IE=edge">
    <meta name="viewport" content=
    "width=device-width, initial-scale=1">
    <link href="http://maxcdn.
    bootstrapcdn.com/bootstrap/3.2.0/css/
    bootstrap.min.css" rel="stylesheet">

    <title>Sign Up</title>
</head>

<body>

    <nav class="navbar navbar-inverse">
        <div class="container-fluid">
            <div class="navbar-header">
                <button type="button" class=
                "navbar-toggle" data-toggle=
                "collapse" data-target=
                "#myNavbar">
                <span class="icon-bar"></span>
                <span class="icon-bar"></span>
                <span class="icon-bar"></span>
                </button>
                <a class="navbar-brand"
                href="#">MyWebsite</a>
            </div>
```

```
<div class="collapse ↵
navbar-collapse" id="myNavbar">

<ul class="nav navbar-nav">
    <li><a href="#">Home</a></li>
    <li><a href="#">Page A</a> ↵
    </li>
    <li><a href="#">Page B</a> ↵
    </li>
    <li class="dropdown">
        <a href="#" class= ↵
        "dropdown-toggle" data- ↵
        toggle="dropdown">Page C ↵
        <b class="caret"></b></a>
        <ul class="dropdown-menu">
            <li><a href="#"> ↵
            Page C - 1</a> </li>
            <li><a href="#"> ↵
            Page C - 2</a> </li>
            <li><a href="#"> ↵
            Page C - 3</a> </li>
        </ul>
    </li>
</ul>

<ul class="nav navbar-nav ↵
navbar-right">
    <li class="active"><a href= ↵
    "#"><span class="glyphicon ↵
    glyphicon-user"></span> ↵
    Sign Up</a></li>
    <li><a href="#"><span class= ↵
    "glyphicon glyphicon-log-in">↵
    </span> Login</a></li>
</ul>

    </div>
  </div>
</nav>

<div class="container">

    <h1>Sign Up</h1>
```

```
<form action="#" method="post">

    <div class="form-group">
        <label for="inputName"> Name
        </label>
        <input type="text" class=
        "form-control" id=
        "inputName" placeholder=
        "Enter your name">
    </div>

    <div class="form-group">
        <label for="inputEmail">
        Email Address</label>
        <input type="email" class=
        "form-control" id=
        "inputName" placeholder=
        "Enter your email address">
    </div>

    <div class="form-group">
        <label for="inputPassword">
        Password</label>
        <input type="password"
        class="form-control" id=
        "inputPassword" >
    </div>

    <div class="form-group">
        <label for=
        "inputRepeatPassword">
        Repeat Password</label>
        <input type="password"
        class="form-control" id=
        "inputRepeatPassword" >
    </div>

    <p><button type="submit" class=
    "btn btn-primary">Submit
    </button></p>

</form>
```

```
    </div>

    <script src="http://code.jquery.com/ ↵
    jquery-1.11.1.min.js"></script>

    <script src="http://maxcdn.bootstrapcdn ↵
    .com/bootstrap/3.2.0/js/ ↵
    bootstrap.min.js "></script>

</body>
</html>
```

Since this is our Sign Up page, we will set the Sign Up button on the top right to active.

Our Sign Up page looks like below:

Figure 9.1

View on browser: http://bit.ly/p-form1
Download: http://bit.ly/dl-form1

9.1 Resizing Input Fields

Looking at the size of the fields above they seem a bit too wide and it would be a good idea to resize them. Let's start by resizing the *Name* field.

Remember this?

```
<div class="col-xs-12 col-sm-12 col-md-6 ↵
            col-lg-3">
```

We have used it before to create a multicolumn layout and to determine how the layout should be displayed on various screen sizes. The same method is used here to control our field's width.

We don't want the fields in our form to be too wide when they are displayed on large and medium screens. On small screens however, we would like the fields to be as wide as possible to make it easy to fill out. How do we do this?

```
...
<div class="row">
    <div class="col-md-4 col-lg-4">
        <div class="form-group">
            <label for="inputName"> ↵
            Name</label>
            <input type="text" class= ↵
            "form-control" id="inputName" ↵
            placeholder="Enter your name">
        </div>
    </div>
</div>
...
```

Explanation:

`<div class="col-md-4 col-lg-4">` indicates the size that we have selected for when the page is viewed on medium (md) and large (lg) screen. For the small and extra small screens we want all the fields to be as wide as possible. Bootstrap does that by default so we do not need to do anything.

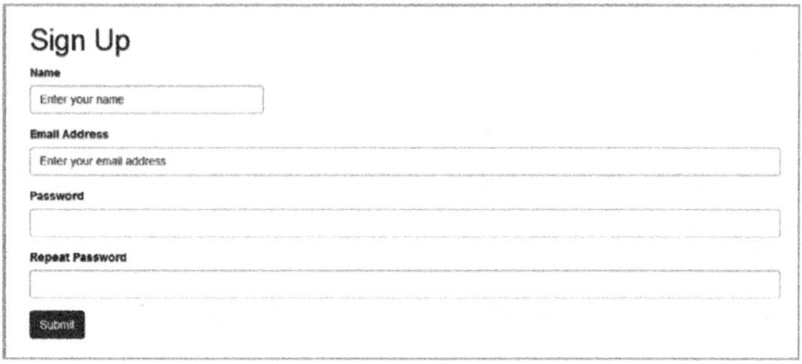

Figure 9.2

Our *Name* field is now narrower than the rest, as expected. Let's see how it looks on a small screen:

Figure 9.3

The *Name* field is back to having the same width as the rest. Why? Because we only set the width for medium (col-md-4) and large (col-lg-4) screens.

So far we have only resized the *Name* field. Let's work on the others.

If we want all fields to be of the same size as the Name field, we can just wrap them all inside the `<div class="row">` and `<div class="col-md-4 col-lg-4">`.

We, however, want to have different widths for different fields. We will make the email address field narrower than the Name field, and the password fields narrower than the email address field. For that we will use `<div class="col-md-3 col-lg-3">` and `<div class="col-md-2 col-lg-2">` respectively.

This is how the page looks on a large screen:

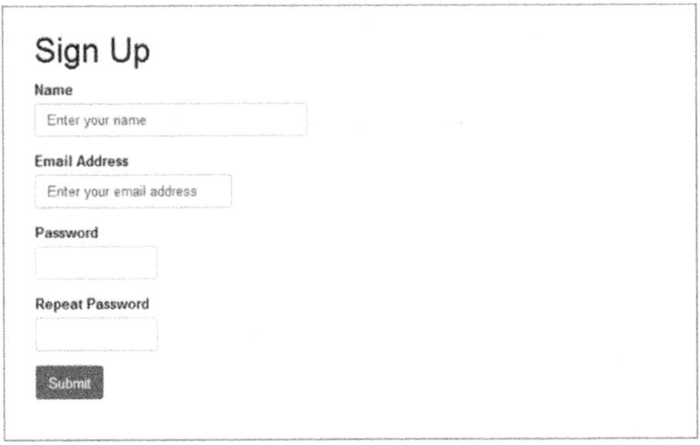

Figure 9.4

Looks good. We'll keep it this way.

How does it look on a small screen? Still the same as seen in Figure 9.3, as expected.

View on browser: http://bit.ly/p-form2
Download: http://bit.ly/dl-form2

One thing we also need to do is to update the Sign Up button in our main page (*index.html*). Now that we have created the Sign Up page (*signup.html*), we should link the Sign Up button to it.

See below:

```
...
<ul class="nav navbar-nav navbar-right">

    <li>
        <a href="signup.html"><span class= ↵
        "glyphicon glyphicon-user"></span> ↵
        Sign Up</a>
    </li>

    <li>
        <a href="#"><span class="glyphicon ↵
        glyphicon-log-in"></span> Login</a>
    </li>

</ul>
...
```

9.2 Form Validation

In form processing, it would be a good idea to make sure that the required fields are not left blank and that the data entered is valid. In short, we need to validate our input.

For our Sign Up page, we would like to make sure that:

1. All the fields are populated.

2. The email address is entered in the valid format.

3. The Password and Repeat Password are the same.

How do we do this? Some JQuery programming will be needed here. If we look at the bottom of our page's HTML, we will see:

```
...
<script src=https://code.jquery.com/ ↵
jquery-1.11.1.js></script>

<script src=http://maxcdn.bootstrapcdn.com/ ↵
bootstrap/3.2.0/js/bootstrap.min.js></script>

    </body>
</html>
```

We will place our JQuery programming right before the `</body>` tag. Let's start by validating the *Name* field:

```
<script>
    $(document).ready(function() {
        $("#submitButton").click(function(e){
            if($("#inputName").val()==""){
                e.preventDefault();
                $("#inputNameFormGroup").
                addClass("has-error");
            }
```

```
        else {
            $("#signupForm").submit();
        }
    });
  });
</script>
```

Explanation:

the `$(document).ready(...)` is used to make sure that our HTML document is completely loaded by the browser before the JQuery is executed. We will use this whenever we use JQuery.

`$("#submitButton").click(...)`, as the code suggests, will run something in the event the submit button is clicked. What will it run? The test to see whether the *Name* field is blank or not. Our *Name* field is given an ID *inputName*, therefore:

```
if($("#inputName").val()==""){

    Do something

}
```

The line can be translated as: "If *inputName* is empty, do something." What should we do when the field Name is empty?

First, we put `preventDefault()`, which prevents the form from submitting. Why? Because we have an error and the form should not be submitted.

Second, we would like to highlight the label *Name* and the border of the input field with a red color. This way the user's attention will be drawn to them.

Bootstrap provides us with a class for this. It is called: `has-error`.

Remember how we wrap the label and the input in one form-group? Since we want to change the color of both the label and the input field, we can target both by using this form-group. The ID of this form group is *inputNameFormGroup*.

Therefore, when the *Name* field is blank, use:

```
$("#inputNameFormGroup").addClass("has-
error");
```

On the other hand, if it is not blank, we will submit the form:

```
else {

    $("#signupForm").submit();

}
```

Done! Now let's test our form. Open the Sign Up page and click the submit button without typing anything.

Since the *Name* field is empty, the label *Name* and the corresponding field are highlighted red. (Since it is a black and white book, the highlight may not be very obvious in the screenshot below.)

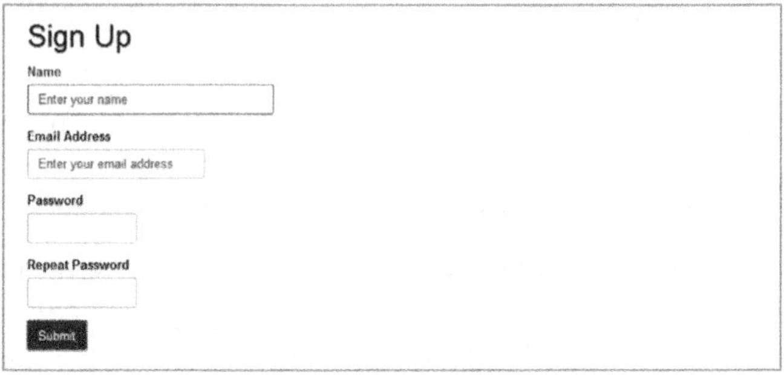

Figure 9.5

At this point we are not yet validating the rest of the fields. Let's do that now.

```
<script>

    $(document).ready(function() {

    var emailReg=/^\w+([\.-]?\w+)*@\w+ ↵
    ([\.-]?\w+)*(\.\w+)+$/;

    $("#submitButton").click(function(e){

        if($("#inputName").val()==""){
            e.preventDefault();
            $("#inputNameFormGroup"). ↵
            addClass("has-error");
        }

        else if($("#inputEmail").val() ↵
        ==""){
            e.preventDefault();
            $("#inputEmailFormGroup") ↵
            .addClass("has-error");
        }
```

```
    else if(!emailReg.test
    ($("#inputEmail").val())){
        e.preventDefault();
        $("#inputEmailFormGroup").
        addClass("has-error");
    }

    else if($("#inputPassword").
    val()==""){
        e.preventDefault();
        $("#inputPasswordFormGroup").
        addClass("has-error");
    }

    else if($("#inputRepeatPassword").
    val()==""){
        e.preventDefault();
        $("#inputRepeatPasswordForm
        Group").addClass("has-error");
    }

    else if($("#inputPassword").
    val()!=$("#inputRepeatPassword").
    val()){
            e.preventDefault();
            $("#inputPasswordFormGroup").
            addClass("has-error");
            $("#inputRepeatPasswordForm
            Group").addClass("has-error");
        }
        else {
            $("#signupForm").submit();
        }
    });
});
```

</script>

Explanation:

In addition to making sure that all fields are not empty, we also do the following:

1. We validate the email address using the following regular expressions:

```
var emailReg = /^\w+([\.-]?\w+)*@\w+([\.-
]?\w+)*(\.\w+)+$/;
```

And we use it here:

```
else if ↵
(!emailReg.test($("#inputEmail").val())){

    e.preventDefault();
    $("#inputEmailFormGroup").addClass("has- ↵
    error");

}
```

Note:
We will not discuss regular expressions in this book. To find out more, you can search the web using the term regular expression, or regex.

2. We are checking whether the password and the repeat password are the same:

```
else if($("#inputPassword").val()!=

    $("#inputRepeatPassword").val()){
        if not the same, do something
    });

}
```

If they are not the same, we would prevent the submission and add the `has-error` class to both *Password* and *Repeat Password* field.

View on browser: http://bit.ly/p-formvld
Download: http://bit.ly/dl-formvld

9.3 Alerts

This would be a good time to introduce the Alert feature provided by Bootstrap. Let's say in addition to highlighting the fields when a validation error is identified, we also would like to display a message to explain to users what the problem is.

For example, when the *Password* and *Repeat Password* are not the same, we would like to display a message that says so.

Something that looks like this:

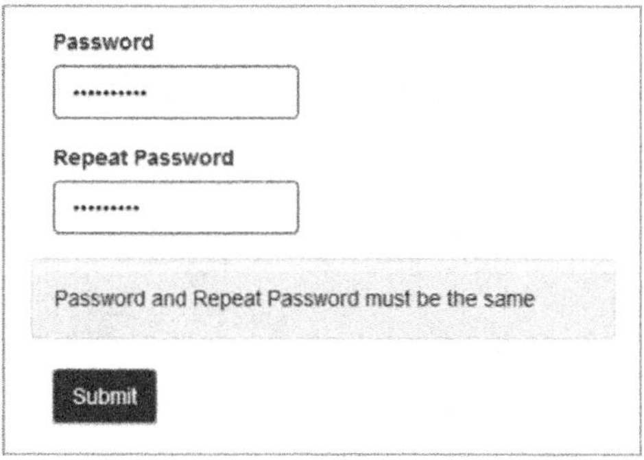

Figure 9.6

First we need to decide where we are going to place the Alert. Let's display it below the fields and above the Submit button. We give this space an ID: *placeForAlert*.

```
...
<div class="row">
    <div class="col-md-2 col-lg-2">
        <div class="form-group" ↵
        id="inputRepeatPasswordFormGroup">
            <label class="control-label" ↵
            for="inputRepeatPassword"> ↵
            Repeat Password</label>
            <input type="password" class= ↵
            "form-control" ↵
            id="inputRepeatPassword">
        </div>
    </div>
</div>

<div class="row">
    <div class="col-md-4 col-lg-4" ↵
    id="placeForAlert"></div>
</div>

<p><button type="submit" class="btn btn- ↵
primary" id="submitButton">Submit</button></p>
...
```

We then add two lines to our JQuery codes:

```
...
else if($("#inputPassword").val()!= ↵
$("#inputRepeatPassword").val()){

    $("#inputPasswordFormGroup").addClass ↵
    ("has-error");
    $("#inputRepeatPasswordFormGroup"). ↵
    addClass("has-error");
```

```
$("#placeForAlert").addClass("alert ↵
alert-warning");
("#placeForAlert").html("Password and ↵
Repeat Password must be the same");

}
...
```

View on browser: http://bit.ly/p-formalert
Download: http://bit.ly/dl-formalert

To test it, refresh the page and fill out the form properly, except for the *Password* and *Repeat Password* field: We need to enter two different values in order to trigger the alert.

9.4 Dismissible Alerts

We can also make the alert dismissible, by adding:

```
$("#placeForAlert").addClass("alert alert-
warning alert-dismissable");
```

And add the x button next to the text:

```
$("#placeForAlert").html("<button type= ↵
'button' class='close' data-dismiss= ↵
'alert'><span class='glyphicon glyphicon- ↵
remove'></span></button> Password and ↵
Repeat Password must be the same");
```

The alert will look like below:

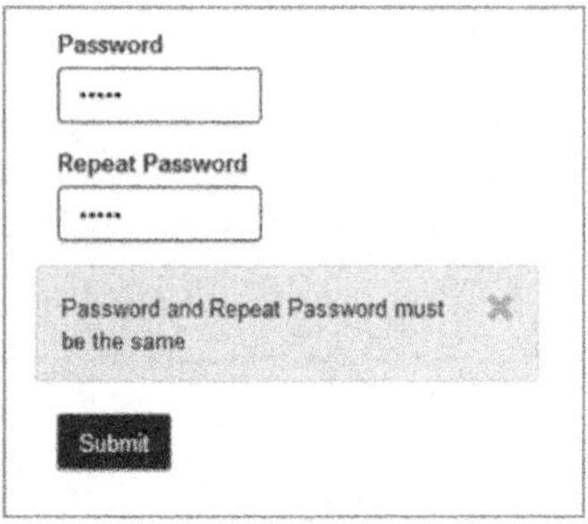

Figure 9.7

View on browser: http://bit.ly/p-formdis
Download: http://bit.ly/dl-formdis

10

MODAL

Modal is a secondary window that when opened prevents us from interacting with the primary window.

As an example we will create a login dialog box that will pop up when the *Login* button is clicked. The end result will look like this:

Figure 10.1

Let's go back to our main page (*index.html*). Add

the following at the bottom of the page, right above the links to the CDNs.

```
<div class="modal-fade" id="loginModal" ↵
tabindex="-1">

    <div class="modal-dialog">

        <div class="modal-content">

            <div class="modal-header">
                (put modal header here)
            </div>

            <div class="modal-body">
                (put modal body here)
            </div>

            <div class="modal-footer">
                (put modal footer here)
            </div>

        </div>

    </div>

</div>
```

We give this modal dialog box the ID of *loginModal*.

A Modal dialog box consists of three parts: A header, a body and a footer.

The header is where we put the *Login* title and the x button to close the box. The body is where we put the login form, and the footer is where the *Cancel* and *Login* buttons are.

The modal header:

```
<div class="modal-header">

    <button type="button" class="close" ↵
    data-dismiss="modal">&times;</button>

    <h4 class="modal-title" id= ↵
    "loginModalLabel">Login</h4>

</div>
```

The modal body:

```
<div class="modal-body">

    <div class="form-group" id= ↵
    "inputUserIDFormGroup">

        <label class="control-label" ↵
        for="inputUserID">User ID</label>

        <input type="text" class="form- ↵
        control" id="inputUserID" ↵
        placeholder="Enter your user ID">

    </div>

    <div class="form-group" id= ↵
    "inputPasswordFormGroup">

        <label class="control-label" ↵
        for="inputPassword">Password</label>

        <input type="password" class="form- ↵
        control" id="inputPassword" ↵
        placeholder="Enter your password">
```

```
    </div>
</div>
```

Since you have been presented with lessons on Forms in Chapter 9, this should look familiar to you by now. It is a form, containing fields for users to enter their *User ID* and *Password*. We will call this our *Login* form.

The modal footer:

```
<div class="modal-footer">

    <button type="button" class="btn btn- ↵
    default" data-dismiss="modal">Cancel ↵
    </button>

    <button type="submit" class="btn ↵
    btn-primary">Login</button>

</div>
```

This is where we display our buttons: The *Cancel* button to close the modal window, and the *Login* button to submit the form.

Since our modal is a form, we should put it inside the `<form>`...`</form>`:

```
<form action="#" method="post" id="loginForm">
    (our modal here)
</form>
```

Lastly, we should modify our *Login* button inside

the navigation bar in order for it to open the modal window when clicked.

```
...
<ul class="nav navbar-nav navbar-right">

    <li><a href="#"><span class="glyphicon ↵
    glyphicon-user"></span> Sign Up</a></li>

    <li><a href="#" data-toggle="modal" ↵
    data-target="#loginModal"><span class= ↵
    "glyphicon glyphicon-log-in"></span> ↵
    Login</a></li>

</ul>
...
```

Reload the page, click the *Login* button and we will see:

Figure 10.2

View on browser: http://bit.ly/p-mdl
Download: http://bit.ly/dl-mdl

OK, the login dialog box may not need to be that big. Luckily, we can have two different sizes for modal: Large or small. Just add `modal-lg` for large or `modal-sm` for small to the `<div class="modal-dialog">`, so it becomes: `<div class="modal-dialog modal-lg">` for big, or `<div class="modal-dialog modal-sm">` for small.

Let's pick the size small:

Figure 10.3

Done!

View on browser: http://bit.ly/p-mdlsm
Download: http://bit.ly/dl-mdlsm

11

WORKING WITH IMAGES

It is time to put an image in our page. Below is the HTML tag for displaying an image:

```
<img src="filename.jpg"/>
```

Let's place it in the first column of our page:

```
<div class="col-xs-12 col-sm-12 col-md-6 ↵
col-lg-3">

    <p><img src="filename.jpg"/></p>
    <p>Paragraph 1...</p>

</div>
```

Figure 11.1 shows what the page looks like on a large screen. The image is too large for the column. Ideally, our image should be responsive to the available space and resize itself to fit in it instead of overlapping with the next column.

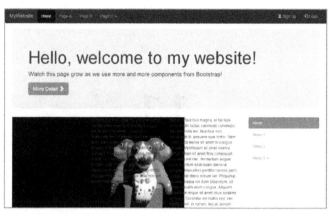

Figure 11.1

In order to make the image responsive, we use the class `img-responsive`.

```
<img class="img-responsive" src= ↵
filename.jpg"/>
```

Let's see how it looks now:

Figure 11.2

View on browser: http://bit.ly/p-img
Download: http://bit.ly/dl-img

That's better. What about when it is viewed on small and medium screens?

On a small screen:

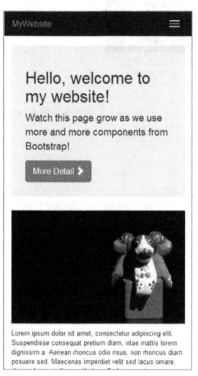

Figure 11.3

The image resizes itself quite nicely.

Let's see how it is on a medium screen:

Figure 11.4

Wait. there is an empty space in the second column. Isn't that a problem?

Yes and no. Remember the column reset?

```
<div class="clearfix visible-**"></div>
```

We used it when we worked on the multi-column layout. With it we set the height of the row to follow the tallest member.

In our example here the tallest member of the first row is the image plus the first paragraph. The second paragraph does not have as much content, therefore the rest of its space is empty.

Figure 11.5

From that perspective, the page does what it is supposed to do. But if you don't like it, you can remove the column reset and see if the page rearranges itself any better.

There is one potential problem that you should be aware of when working with images. When the width of the image is less than the width of the space, the image will be displayed aligned to the left instead of the center.

If you find yourself in this situation and you would like to have your image centered, Bootstrap provides a helper class to center it:

```
class="center-block"
```

To use it, just add it to the class that we have:

```
<img class="img-responsive center-block"
src="filename.jpg"/>
```

and our image will be centered at all times.

Bootstrap also provides some classes to style our image:

We can give it rounded corners:

```
<img class="img-responsive img-rounded"
src="filename.jpg"/>
```

Figure 11.6

Or give it rounded borders:

```
<img class="img-responsive img-thumbnail"
src="filename.jpg"/>
```

Figure 11.7

Or give it a round shape:

```
<img class="img-responsive img-circle"  ↵
src="filename.jpg"/>
```

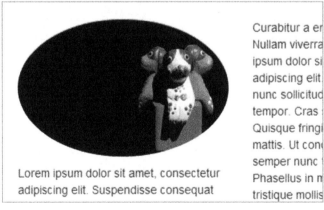

Figure 11.8

12

TABLES

We will start our lesson by creating a simple table below.

```
<table>
    <thead>
        <tr>
            <th>Header 1</th>
            <th>Header 2</th>
            <th>Header 3</th>
        </tr>
    </thead>
    <tbody>
        <tr>
            <td>Row 1 Column 1</td>
            <td>Row 1 Column 2</td>
            <td>Row 1 Column 3</td>
        </tr>
        <tr>
            <td>Row 2 Column 1</td>
            <td>Row 2 Column 2</td>
            <td>Row 2 Column 3</td>
        </tr>
        <tr>
            <td>Row 3 Column 1</td>
            <td>Row 3 Column 2</td>
```

```
        <td>Row 3 Column 3</td>
     </tr>
   </tbody>
</table>
```

The table will look like this:

Header 1   **Header 2**   **Header 3**
Row 1 Column 1Row 1 Column 2Row 1 Column 3
Row 2 Column 1Row 2 Column 2Row 2 Column 3
Row 3 Column 1Row 3 Column 2Row 3 Column 3

Figure 12.1

It does not look like much just yet. Let's style it further using Bootstrap. We will use:

```
<table class="table">
...
</table>
```

It will transform our table into:

Header 1	Header 2	Header 3
Row 1 Column 1	Row 1 Column 2	Row 1 Column 3
Row 2 Column 1	Row 2 Column 2	Row 2 Column 3
Row 3 Column 1	Row 3 Column 2	Row 3 Column 3

Figure 12.2

To give borders, we use table-bordered:

```
<table class="table table-bordered">
...
</table>
```

Header 1	Header 2	Header 3
Row 1 Column 1	Row 1 Column 2	Row 1 Column 3
Row 2 Column 1	Row 2 Column 2	Row 2 Column 3
Row 3 Column 1	Row 3 Column 2	Row 3 Column 3

Figure 12.3

We can add alternate shading (known as zebra-striping) to increase legibility:

```
<table class="table table-striped">
...
</table>
```

Header 1	Header 2	Header 3
Row 1 Column 1	Row 1 Column 2	Row 1 Column 3
Row 2 Column 1	Row 2 Column 2	Row 2 Column 3
Row 3 Column 1	Row 3 Column 2	Row 3 Column 3

Figure 12.4

We can also make the rows to change color when our mouse pointer hovers over them:

```
<table class="table table-hover">
...
</table>
```

Although in the example above each of the classes are used separately, we can also use them all on one table.

We can do:

```
<table class="table table-bordered table-
striped table-hover">
...
</table>
```

View on browser: http://bit.ly/p-tbl
Download: http://bit.ly/dl-tbl

12.1 Setting the Width of the Table

You must have noticed that when our table is displayed, it takes the maximum available space. This is because the class *table* sets the width of the table to 100%. (meaning it will take 100% of the width of the space available to it).

The problem with this is, when the content is sparse, the table can look awkward, like below:

Name of Produce	Quantity
Apple	3
Orange	10
Strawberry	2

Figure 12.5

It would be better if we can narrow the table's width somehow. How do we do this?

Remember this?

```
<div class="container">
    <div class="row">
```

```
        <div class="col-md-4">
            ...
        </div>
    </div>
</div>
```

That's right. We used it to create a multi-column layout. We can utilize that same method here. Simply put our table inside it:

```
<div class="container">
    <div class="row">
        <div class="col-md-4">
            <table class="table table-  ↵
            bordered table-striped  ↵
            table-hover">
                ...
            </table>
        </div>
    </div>
</div>
```

Now our table does not occupy the whole space anymore:

Name of Produce	Quantity
Apple	3
Orange	10
Strawberry	2

Figure 12.6

What if we want to move our table to the middle?

Remember that with the grid system we can create

up to 12 columns? With `col-md-4` we can put one
column of the same size on the left, and another on
the right, and our table will be nicely tucked in the
middle.

```
<div class="container">
    <div class="row">
        <div class="col-md-4"></div>
        <div class="col-md-4">
            <table class="table table- ↵
            bordered table-striped ↵
            table-hover">
                ...
            </table>
        </div>
        <div class="col-md-4"></div>
    </div>
</div>
```

This of course is not how the grid system is
intended to be used. There is a better way:

We can use *Offset*. Notice that in the above
example, we pretty much 'push' our table to the
middle by using two empty columns of the same
size. Using offset we can create the same effect
without the empty columns:

```
<div class="container">
    <div class="row">
        <div class="col-md-4 col-md-offset-4">
            <table class="table table- ↵
            bordered table-striped ↵
            table-hover">
                ...
```

```
        </table>
      </div>
    </div>
</div>
```

Note:

As you may remember, the `class col-md-*` *that we use above will work for a medium-sized screen (*`md`*). This means, if you view the page on a small screen, the table will be back to occupying 100% of the width.*

12.2 Setting the Width of the Column

By default, the width of the columns in our table is set automatically. But we can change it. As an example, let's make the second column of our table as narrow as possible, while leaving the first column to adjust automatically.

We use the same method, except this time we apply it to the column:

```
<table class="table table-bordered table- ↵
striped table-hover">

    <thead>
        <tr>
            <th>Name of Produce</th>
            <th class="col-md-1">Qty</th>
        </tr>
    </thead>

    <tbody>
        <tr>
            <td>Apple</td>
            <td>3</td>
```

```
        </tr>
           ...
    </tbody>

</table>
```

Name of Produce	Qty
Apple	3
Orange	10
Strawberry	2

Figure 12.7

12.3 Table's Text Alignment

In the example above, the headers of the table are aligned to the left. Let's center them. While we are at it, let's also align the content of the second column to the right. For this we need what Bootstrap calls *Alignment Classes*.

To center the text we use text-center. To align to the right: text-right.

```
<table class="table table-bordered table-
striped table-hover">
    <thead>
        <tr>
            <th class="text-center">
                Name of Produce
            </th>
            <th class="col-md-1 text-center">
                Qty
            </th>
        </tr>
```

107

```
    </thead>

    <tbody>
        <tr>
            <td>Apple</td>
            <td class="text-right">3</td>
        </tr>
        <tr>
            <td>Orange</td>
            <td class="text-right">10</td>
        </tr>
        <tr>
            <td>Strawberry</td>
            <td class="text-right">2</td>
        </tr>
    </tbody>

</table>
```

Note:
Other than `text-center` *and* `text-right` *we also have* `text-left`, `text-justify` *(all lines have equal width) and* `text-nowrap` *(the text does not automatically break into new lines).*

Name of Produce	Qty
Apple	3
Orange	10
Strawberry	2

Figure 12.8

Before we end this chapter, let's incorporate the table above into our *index.html* page. We will place it in the second column. Since the space is limited to begin with, we will leave the table's width to fill

100% of the column's width.

```
<div class="container">
    <div class="jumbotron">
        <h1>Hello, welcome to my website!</h1>
        <p>Watch this page grow as we use
        more and more components from
        Bootstrap!</p>

        <a href="#" class="btn btn-primary
        btn-lg">More Detail <span class=
        "glyphicon glyphicon-chevron-right">
        </span></a>
    </div>
</div>

<div class="container">
    <div class="row">

        <div class="col-xs-12 col-sm-12
        col-md-6 col-lg-3">
            <p><img class="img-responsive
            center-block" src=
            "sampleimage_1.jpg"></p>
            <p>Paragraph 1...</p>
        </div>

        <div class="col-xs-12 col-sm-12
        col-md-6 col-lg-3">

            <table class="table table-
            bordered table-striped table-
            hover">
                ...
            </table>

                <p>Paragraph 2...</p>

        </div>

...
```

Figure 12.9

View on browser: http://bit.ly/p-tbl2
Download: http://bit.ly/dl-tbl2

13

LIGHT CUSTOMIZATION

Developing a website using Bootstrap's default style is of course only half the battle. Ultimately we would like to have a unique style that we can call our own. In this chapter we will show you how to easily customize Bootstrap using what is called a light customization.

Here is what we are going to customize: Currently our Jumbotron has a gray background color and black text. We will try to change them. If you remember, this is the question we have when we were working on Jumbotron in Chapter 4 (Page 23).

Let's see how this is done. We will use our *index.html* that we have worked on so far (as seen in figure 13.1) as the starting point.

The following are the steps we need to take to perform our customization:

Figure 13.1

Step 1: Identify the component that we would like to customize.

In this case, we would like to customize the Jumbotron. Below is what we wrote when we put Jumbotron into our page:

```
...
<div class="container">
    <div class="jumbotron">
        <h1>Hello, welcome to my website!</h1>
        <p>Watch this page grow as we use ↵
        more and more components from ↵
        Bootstrap!</p>
        <a href="#" class="btn btn-primary ↵
        btn-lg">More Detail <span class= ↵
        "glyphicon glyphicon-chevron-right"> ↵
        </span></a>
    </div>
</div>
...
```

Notice the use of the class *jumbotron*.

Step 2: Find the corresponding class in the *bootstrap.css* that we downloaded.

If you are using CDNs and have not downloaded the file, this is the time to do so (See page 13). Open the *bootstrap.css* using any file editor and search for the text *"jumbotron"*.

Note:
Make sure you open the bootstrap.css and not the bootstrap.min.css. Although the contents are the same, the latter is the minified or compressed version and can be hard to read.

Here is what we found:

```
.jumbotron {
    padding: 30px;
    margin-bottom: 30px;
    color: inherit;
    background-color: #eee;
}
```

Step 3: Create our own CSS file and copy / paste the above code.

Create a new CSS file. Let's call it *custom.css*. Paste the codes that we found above and save it. Don't forget to link our page to it:

```
<link rel="stylesheet"
href=http://maxcdn.bootstrapcdn.com/↵
bootstrap/3.2.0/css/bootstrap.min.css>

<link rel="stylesheet" href="custom.css">
```

Step 4: Customize it

After we have copied the class to our *custom.css* file, we are ready to make the changes. In the above we can see that the background-color is set to `#eee`, which is a shade of light gray. Let's change it to dark blue. The HTML color code for dark blue is `#00007f`. (there are of course many different shades of blue, which gives us numerous HTML color codes for them. We just pick one as an example).

In our *custom.css* file, change the color code of the background color:

```
.jumbotron {
    padding: 30px;
    margin-bottom: 30px;
    color: inherit;
    background-color: #00007f;
}
```

Save it. Let's see what happens to our page:

Figure 13.2

The background color has changed. But now our text is not legible. Let's fix it by changing the text color to white. We will repeat the customization steps again.

Identify the component that we use to display the text inside the Jumbotron: It is `<h1>` and `<p>`. Searching for them in the *bootstrap.css* we found:

```
.jumbotron h1,
.jumbotron .h1 {
    color: inherit;
}
.jumbotron p {
    margin-bottom: 15px;
    font-size: 21px;
    font-weight: 200;
}
```

Copy them to our *custom.css* and change the color to white (HTML color code: #ffffff).

```
.jumbotron h1,
.jumbotron .h1 {
    color: #ffffff;
}

.jumbotron p {
    margin-bottom: 15px;
    font-size: 21px;
    font-weight: 200;
    color:#ffffff;
}
```

See the result in Figure 13.3.

View on browser: http://bit.ly/p-custom1
Download: http://bit.ly/dl-custom1

Figure 13.3

Let's go further. What if instead of plain dark blue as a background color of the Jumbotron, we want to use a background image instead?

Since we are still working on the Jumbotron and we already have the *jumbotron* class in the *custom.css*, there is no need to copy anything from the *bootstrap.css*. We can make the changes right away:

```
.jumbotron {
    padding: 30px;
    margin-bottom: 30px;
    color: inherit;
    background-image: url('image_file.jpg');
    background-position: center;
}
```

See the result in Figure 13.4.

Note:

1. *You will need to change the file name "image_file.jpg" to the name of the image file that you have.*

2. *The image should be saved in the same folder as the page.*

Figure 13.4

View on browser: http://bit.ly/p-custom2
Download: http://bit.ly/dl-custom2

What about changing the font? In *bootstrap.css*, the font for the page is set in this:

```
body {
    font-family: "Helvetica Neue", ↵
    Helvetica, Arial, sans-serif;
    font-size: 14px;
    line-height: 1.428571429;
    color: #333333;
    background-color: #ffffff;
}
```

Copy the above to our *custom.css*. Let's say we change the font family to:

```
font-family: "Times New Roman", Times, serif;
```

The result below:

Figure 13.5

View on browser: http://bit.ly/p-custom3
Download: http://bit.ly/dl-custom3

Before we end this chapter, let's go back to Chapter 8 "Working with Navigation" (Page 41) where we stumbled upon this issue:

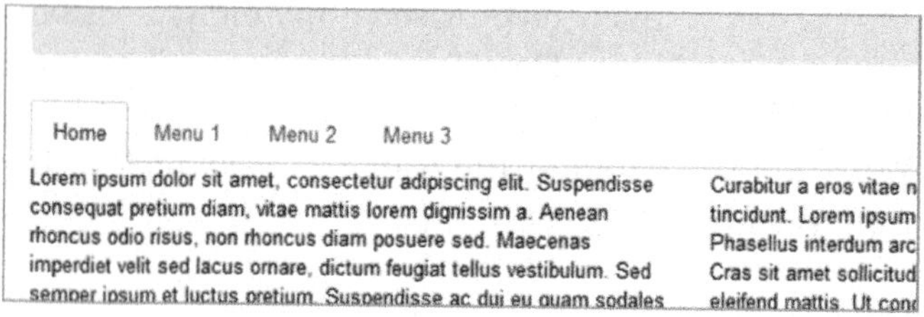

Figure 13.6

The text is placed awfully closed to our Tabs. Let's fix it now.

We know that our text is wrapped inside the container:

```
...
<div class="container">
    <div class="row">
        <div class="col-xs-12 col-sm-12 col- ↵
        md-6 col-lg-3">
            <p>Paragraph 1...</p>
```

```
    </div>
...
```

Search for *"container"* in the *bootstrap.css* to find the following:

```
.container {
    padding-right: 15px;
    padding-left: 15px;
    margin-right: auto;
    margin-left: auto;
}
```

Copy the above to our *custom.css* and add one more line:

```
.container {
    padding-right: 15px;
    padding-left: 15px;
    margin-right: auto;
    margin-left: auto;
    margin-top:20px;
}
```

Let's see what we have:

Figure 13.7

Problem solved!

14

CUSTOMIZATION USING LESS

In this chapter we will attempt the same customization as we did in the previous chapter, except that this time we will do it through the Bootstrap's LESS.

If you have not worked with LESS before, you may want to read Appendix 2 (Page 210) for a quick introduction.

14.1 Customizing Bootstrap's LESS file

In this exercise we will be using the same HTML file and image file that we used in the previous chapter.

We will do the same two customizations: The first one is to change the background and the font color of the Jumbotron. The second is instead of changing the background color, we decide to use a background image instead.

Let's start with the first customization.

To customize the Jumbotron, we need to find its LESS file. When we download and extract the Bootstrap's source code, we will get the following directory:

Figure 14.1

Open the *less* folder and find the *jumbotron.less* file. Open it using any text editor. We will see the following:

```
//
// Jumbotron
// -------------------------------------------


.jumbotron {
  padding: @jumbotron-padding;
  margin-bottom: @jumbotron-padding;
  color: @jumbotron-color;
  background-color: @jumbotron-bg;
...
```

Let's focus on this for now. If you remember, this is similar to the part that we worked on in the previous chapter, which looks like this:

```
.jumbotron {
    padding: 30px;
    margin-bottom: 30px;
    color: inherit;
    background-color: #eee;
}
```

Similar, apart from the parts with the @ sign, right?

So what are `@jumbotron-padding`, `@jumbotron-color` and `@jumbotron-bg`? They are variables, and they are defined in a separate file aptly named *variables.less*.

Open the file and take a peek inside. Use the search function of your text editor and search for *'jumbotron'*. You will find:

```
@jumbotron-padding:          30px;
@jumbotron-color:            inherit;
@jumbotron-bg:               @gray-lighter;
@jumbotron-heading-color:    inherit;
@jumbotron-font-size:        ceil((@font-size-↵
base * 1.5));
```

Looking at the parts highlighted in boldface we can see where the values of Jumbotron's padding, margin-bottom and color came from.

For example:

```
padding: @jumbotron-padding;
```

Where

```
@jumbotron-padding: 30 px;
```

We can therefore conclude that:

```
padding: 30px;
```

What about the `@jumbotron-bg`? Now it has the value of `@gray-lighter`. How did it become `#eee`?

Remember that in LESS we can use a variable to define another variable. In this case, the value of background color is set using the variable `@jumbotron-bg`, and the value of this `@jumbotron-bg` is set by another variable called `@gray-lighter`.

Search the *variables.less* once again for `@gray-lighter`. We will find:

```
@gray-darker:    lighten(#000, 13.5%); // #222
@gray-dark:      lighten(#000, 20%);   // #333
@gray:           lighten(#000, 33.5%); // #555
@gray-light:     lighten(#000, 46.7%); // #777
@gray-lighter:   lighten(#000, 93.5%); // #eee
```

This is called a color operation function. Starting from black (`#000`) as a base, we create several shades of gray by using the function *lighten*. The higher the percentage value, the lighter the shade of gray. The hexadecimal numbers behind the comment sign // are the color code equivalent of the respective shades of gray.

Technically, we can achieve the same result by just doing the following:

```
@gray-darker:    #222;
@gray-dark:      #333;
@gray:           #555;
@gray-light:     #777;
@gray-lighter:   #eee;
```

This however, assumes that you know all the HTML color codes for different shades of gray.

Consider this example. Let's say we want to create another set of color shades, using dark blue (#00007f) as a base. We would start by writing:

```
@blue : #00007f;
```

Let's say after @blue we would like a set of variables to represent lighter shades of blue, in order to have @blue-light, @blue-lighter, and @blue-lightest. We will need to know the hexadecimal color codes for all of them. What is the hexadecimal color code of *something slightly lighter than #00007f* anyway? We will need an HTML color chart for that.

It is much easier to write:

```
@blue :          #00007f;
@blue-light:     lighten(#00007f, 30%);
@blue-lighter:   lighten(#00007f, 60%);
@blue-lightest:  lighten(#00007f, 90%);
```

Note:

The above is just an example of course. Feel free to name the variables whatever you like and choose the base color you like.

When it is compiled, all the color operation functions will be translated into their HTML color codes.

Note: If you are not familiar with compiling LESS, see Appendix 3 (Page 222).

Let's add the above lines into our *variables.less* file. We can put them under the @gray variables:

```
@gray-darker:    lighten(#000, 13.5%); // #222
@gray-dark:      lighten(#000, 20%);   // #333
@gray:           lighten(#000, 33.5%); // #555
@gray-light:     lighten(#000, 46.7%); // #777
@gray-lighter:   lighten(#000, 93.5%); // #eee

@blue :          #00007f;
@blue-light:     lighten(#00007f, 30%);
@blue-lighter:   lighten(#00007f, 60%);
@blue-lightest:  lighten(#00007f, 90%);

@brand-primary: #428bca;
@brand-success: #5cb85c;
@brand-info:    #5bc0de;
@brand-warning: #f0ad4e;
@brand-danger:  #d9534f;
```

Now let's change the background color of our Jumbotron to blue:

```
@jumbotron-padding:        30px;
@jumbotron-color:          inherit;
@jumbotron-bg:             @blue;
```

```
@jumbotron-heading-color:    inherit;
@jumbotron-font-size: ceil((@font-size-base ↵
* 1.5));
```

Save the *variable.less* file.

But wait, we are not done yet. The next step is to change the Jumbotron's text color to make it legible in a dark blue background. Let's go back to the *jumbotron.less* file.

We have the following:

```
.jumbotron {
  padding: @jumbotron-padding;
  margin-bottom: @jumbotron-padding;
  color: @jumbotron-color;
  background-color: @jumbotron-bg;

  h1,
  .h1 {
    color: @jumbotron-heading-color;
  }
  p {
    margin-bottom: (@jumbotron-padding / 2);
    font-size: @jumbotron-font-size;
    font-weight: 200;
  }
}
```

As we learned in the previous chapter, the components that we use to display the text inside the Jumbotron are `<h1>` and `<p>`.

Let's change the color of `<h1>` and `<p>`. Since we have defined some variables to represent some lighter shades of blue, let's use one of them. We will pick the lightest one for our text:

```
h1,
.h1 {
  color: @blue-lightest;
}
p {
  margin-bottom: (@jumbotron-padding / 2);
  font-size: @jumbotron-font-size;
  font-weight: 200;
  color: @blue-lightest;
}
```

Save the *jumbotron.less* file.

Compile the *bootstrap.less* file. The result is a new CSS file. Let's name this file *bootstrap_custom.css*.

Let's see if the compiled file has the customization that we want. Open the newly created *bootstrap_custom.css* and search for *"jumbotron"*:

```
.jumbotron {
  padding: 30px;
  margin-bottom: 30px;
  color: inherit;
  background-color: #00007f;
}
.jumbotron h1,
.jumbotron .h1 {
  color: #ffffff;
}
.jumbotron p {
  margin-bottom: 15px;
  font-size: 21px;
  font-weight: 200;
  color: #ffffff;
}
```

The background color is now set to blue (#00007f) and the color of `<h1>` and `<p>` is now white

(#ffffff). If you remember, this is exactly the same as what we did in the previous chapter, except this time instead of creating another CSS file that contains our customization, we customize Bootstrap's CSS file through LESS.

14.2 Implementing the Customized CSS File

Now that we have our customized Bootstrap CSS file (*bootstrap_custom.css*), we do not need the *custom.css* that we have created before. We also cannot use the CSS file from Bootstrap's CDN anymore, because that file is the original CSS file, not the customized one.

So we will not be using this one:

```
<link href="http://maxcdn.
bootstrapcdn.com/bootstrap/3.2.0/
css/bootstrap.min.css" rel="stylesheet">
```

Remember in Chapter 2 (page 13) we have two options of using Bootstrap, either by using the downloaded files or by using its CDNs?

Since we cannot use Bootstrap's CDN anymore, the easiest way to implement our customized CSS file is by taking the first option, using the downloaded files.

As discussed in Chapter 2, when we download Bootstrap, we will get the following folders: *css*, *fonts* and *js*. We can ignore the *js* folder because we are still using Bootstrap's javascript from its CDN:

```
<script src="http://maxcdn.
bootstrapcdn.com/bootstrap/3.2.0/js/bootstrap.
min.js"></script>
```

That leaves us with the *css* and the *fonts* folders. Make sure our *bootstrap_custom.css* is copied to the *css* folder.

Note:
Make sure the contents of the fonts folder are intact. We need them to display the glyphicons.

Then we need to incorporate this CSS file into our HTML page. In the previous chapter we had the following:

```
<link rel="stylesheet"
href=http://maxcdn.bootstrapcdn.com/bootstrap/
3.2.0/css/bootstrap.min.css>
<link rel="stylesheet" href="custom.css">
```

Let's replace it with our *bootstrap_custom.css*. We will end up with just one line below:

```
<link rel="stylesheet"
href="css/bootstrap_custom.css">
```

And we are done! Test it and our Jumbotron now looks like this:

Figure 14.2

The second customization we tried in the previous chapter was giving the Jumbotron a background image. Let's see how we do this with LESS:

We will use the same background image that we used in the previous chapter. Let's visit the *jumbotron.less* file again:

```
.jumbotron {
  padding: @jumbotron-padding;
  margin-bottom: @jumbotron-padding;
  color: @jumbotron-color;
  background-color: @jumbotron-bg;
```

Change it to:

```
.jumbotron {
  padding: @jumbotron-padding;
  margin-bottom: @jumbotron-padding;
  color: @jumbotron-color;
  background-image: url('../image_file.jpg');
  background-position: center;
```

Replace the *image_file.jpg* with your image's file

name, and make sure that the image file is stored in the same folder as the HTML file.

We are done! Compile the *bootstrap.less* and make sure the resulting CSS file is saved in the *css* folder.

Note:

Notice the difference between the light and LESS customization when it comes to setting the background image. In light customization we wrote: `background-image: url('image_file.jpg');` *while in LESS customization we wrote:* `background-image: url('../image_file.jpg');`

This is because in light customization we are using Bootstrap's CDN and therefore we do not have the css folder. In LESS customization, we put the custom CSS file inside the css folder. Since the image is in the root folder, we need to use "../" for the CSS to point to the image's location.

Figure 14.3

14.3 Why LESS?

Some of you may ask: if we can do the same customization using the light customization method, why bother using a more complicated method such as LESS?

If what we need involves minimum customization, we are probably better off by going the light-customization route. We can benefit from using Bootstrap's CDN and an additional small CSS file will not adversely affect our site's performance.

However, the more customization we do, the bigger our custom CSS file will be. If you have downloaded Bootstrap's CSS file, you probably have noticed that the file is more than 100kB in size. That is a big file. If on top of that we have another big file for our customization, our website will get even heavier and costlier to load.

Furthermore, by customizing LESS, we can pick and choose the components that we are going to use, and drop the ones we do not need. This will reduce the CSS file size further.

To illustrate this point, let's open the *bootstrap.less* file and see the content. Inside, we will see a list of Bootstrap components:

```
// Components
@import "component-animations.less";
@import "dropdowns.less";
@import "button-groups.less";
@import "input-groups.less";
@import "navs.less";
@import "navbar.less";
@import "breadcrumbs.less";
@import "pagination.less";
@import "pager.less";
@import "labels.less";
@import "badges.less";
@import "jumbotron.less";
@import "thumbnails.less";
@import "alerts.less";
@import "progress-bars.less";
@import "media.less";
@import "list-group.less";
@import "panels.less";
@import "responsive-embed.less";
@import "wells.less";
@import "close.less";

// Components w/ JavaScript
@import "modals.less";
@import "tooltip.less";
@import "popovers.less";
@import "carousel.less";
```

If we do not need to use all of the components, we can drop them by commenting them out. Let's say we have decided that we will not use the following components on our site: breadcrumb, pagination, badges, and wells:

```
@import "component-animations.less";
@import "dropdowns.less";
@import "button-groups.less";
@import "input-groups.less";
@import "navs.less";
@import "navbar.less";
//@import "breadcrumbs.less";
```

```less
//@import "pagination.less";
@import "pager.less";
@import "labels.less";
//@import "badges.less";
@import "jumbotron.less";
@import "thumbnails.less";
@import "alerts.less";
@import "progress-bars.less";
@import "media.less";
@import "list-group.less";
@import "panels.less";
@import "responsive-embed.less";
//@import "wells.less";
@import "close.less";

// Components w/ JavaScript
@import "modals.less";
@import "tooltip.less";
@import "popovers.less";
@import "carousel.less";
```

If we recompile the *boostrap.less* file, the resulting CSS file will be smaller in size, thus lighter to load.

Another obvious reason to use LESS is its ease of maintenance. The more customization we do, the more we will have to maintain. By using the features available in LESS such as variables, nested rules and so forth, the maintenance of the CSS file will be a lot simpler. Refer to Appendix 2 (Page 210) for more details.

15

CAROUSEL

Carousel can make a page more lively with images sliding in and out in a timely fashion. As an exercise we will transform our Jumbotron into a Carousel.

The end result will look like below:

Figure 15.1

Carousel can be broken down into three parts: The

Indicators, the Slides and the Controls.

The Indicators are the three little circles at the bottom of the Carousel. They indicate which slide is being displayed at that particular moment. (We have three circles because in this example we will have three slides.)

The Slides are the images that slide in and out when we click the left or right arrow. They also slide automatically when the page is idle.

The Controls are the arrows located on the left and right of the slide.

Let's create our Carousel. Open the *index.html* and replace the Jumbotron with the following:

```html
<div id="mycarousel" class="carousel slide" ↵
data-ride="carousel">

    <ol class="carousel-indicators">
        <li data-target="#mycarousel" ↵
        data-slide-to="0" class="active"></li>
        <li data-target="#mycarousel" ↵
        data-slide-to="1"></li>
        <li data-target="#mycarousel" ↵
        data-slide-to="2"></li>
    </ol>

    <div class="carousel-inner">
        <div class="item active">
            <div class="slide1"></div>
                <div class="carousel-caption">
                    <h1>Hello, welcome to my ↵
                    website!</h1>
```

```
            <p>Watch this page grow ↵
            as we use more and more ↵
            components from ↵
            Bootstrap!</p>
            <p><a href="#" class=" ↵
            btn btn-primary btn-sm"> ↵
            More Detail </a></p>
        </div>
    </div>

    <div class="item">
        <div class="slide2"></div>
        <div class="carousel-caption">
        <h1>It's a breeze.</h1>
        <p>Develop great looking ↵
        website quickly and easily!↵
        </p>
    </div>

</div>

<div class="item">
    <div class="slide3"></div>
    <div class="carousel-caption">
        <h1>And it's responsive ↵
        too.</h1>
        <p>Create a website that ↵
        looks great on any device</p>
    </div>
</div>
</div>

<a class="left carousel-control" ↵
href="#mycarousel" data-slide="prev"> ↵
<span class="glyphicon glyphicon- ↵
chevron-left"></span></a>
<a class="right carousel-control" ↵
href="#mycarousel" data-slide=↵"next"> ↵
<span class="glyphicon glyphicon- ↵
chevron-right"></span></a>

</div>
```

Explanation:

We put the Carousel inside the following:

```
<div id="mycarousel" class="carousel slide" ↵
data-ride="carousel">
    ...
</div>
```

As you can see above, we give this Carousel the ID:
mycarousel.

Then we have the indicators:

```
<ol class="carousel-indicators">
    <li data-target="#mycarousel" ↵
    data-slide-to="0" class="active"></li>
    <li data-target="#mycarousel" ↵
    data-slide-to="1"></li>
    <li data-target="#mycarousel" ↵
    data-slide-to="2"></li>
</ol>
```

We are going to display three slides, hence the
three indicators. The first indicator is set to active
as a default. When the page is opened, the default
slide will be shown first.

Below that we have the codes for the slides. There
are three items for the three slides. The first item is
set to active as a default.

```
<div class="item active">
    <div class="slide1"></div>
    ...
</div>
```

Each item has a caption. This is where we put our text. In this example the captions consist of a heading (<h1>) and a paragraph (<p>).

```
<div class="carousel-caption">
    <h1>Hello, welcome to my website!</h1>
    <p>Watch this page grow as we use more ↵
    and more components from Bootstrap! </p>
    <p><a href="#" class="btn btn-primary ↵
    btn-sm">More Detail</a></p>
</div>
```

How do we set the images to be displayed as slides? That is where the customization comes in. Since we have learned both the light-customization and customization using LESS, we will show both.

15.1 Carousel – Light customization

We will be reusing the *custom.css* file that we created before in Chapter 13.

In our Carousel we will have three slides, with each having its unique background image. As you can see below, each item represents a slide, and for each slide we have a class *slide1*, *slide2* and *slide3* that we need to define in our *custom.css*.

```
<div class="carousel-inner">
    <div class="item active">
        <div class="slide1"></div>
        <div class="carousel-caption">
            ...
        </div>
    </div>
</div>
```

```
    <div class="item">
        <div class="slide2"></div>
        <div class="carousel-caption">
            ...
        </div>
    </div>
    <div class="item">
        <div class="slide3"></div>
        <div class="carousel-caption">
            ...
        </div>
    </div>
</div>
```

In our *custom.css* these *slide1*, *slide2* and *slide3* classes will be defined as follows:

```
.slide1 {
    background-image: url('image_1.jpg');
    height:500px;
    background-repeat: no-repeat;
    background-position: center;
    background-size: cover;
}
.slide2 {
    background-image: url('image_2.jpg');
    height:500px;
    background-repeat: no-repeat;
    background-position: center;
    background-size: cover;

}
.slide3 {
    background-image: url('image_3.jpg');
    height:500px;
    background-repeat: no-repeat;
    background-position: center;
    background-size: cover;

}
```

That is how we display the images inside the Carousel. Obviously we need to put the image files in the same folder as the page.

While we are at it, let's make the fonts for the text a little bigger:

```
.carousel-caption h1 {
    font-size:60px;
}

.carousel-caption p {
    font-size:20px;
}
```

Save it and let's have a look at the result:

Figure 15.2

Looks good, except that there is a rather wide white line separating the carousel from the navigation bar. What if we don't want that line to be that wide?

That line appears there because our navigation bar

has a default bottom margin. If we want to set our own bottom margin for the navigation bar, we can add to the *custom.css* the following:

```
.navbar {
    margin-bottom: 1px;
}
```

Let's see the result now:

Figure 15.3

We are done!

View on browser: http://bit.ly/p-crsl
Download: http://bit.ly/dl-crsl

15.2 Carousel – Using LESS

In order to do the same customization as above using LESS, we need to open *carousel.less*.

At the end of the file we will add the following:

```
.slide1 {
    background-image: url('../image_1.jpg');
    height:500px;
    background-repeat: no-repeat;
    background-position: center;
    background-size: cover;
}

.slide2 {
    background-image: url('../image_2.jpg');
    height:500px;
    background-repeat: no-repeat;
    background-position: center;
    background-size: cover;

}

.slide3 {
    background-image: url('../image_3.jpg');
    height:500px;
    background-repeat: no-repeat;
    background-position: center;
    background-size: cover;

}
```

This, however, is not taking full advantage of what LESS can do. Do you see a repetitive pattern on the above code? There is a more efficient way of doing it. It is time to introduce ourselves to *mixins*.

Let's rewrite the above using *mixins*:

```
.slideimage {
height:500px;
background-repeat: no-repeat;
background-position: center;
background-size: cover;
```

```
}

.slide1 {
background-image: url('../image_1.jpg');
.slideimage;
}

.slide2 {
background-image: url('../image_2.jpg');
.slideimage;
}

.slide3 {
background-image: url('../image_3.jpg');
.slideimage;
}
```

Now we do not have any repetitive lines.

Let's enlarge the text inside the Carousel. In the light customization method, we did the following:

```
.carousel-caption h1 {
    font-size:60px;
}

.carousel-caption p {
    font-size:20px;
}
```

In *carousel.less* we can do the same thing. First, find the part that contains *.carousel-caption*:

```
.carousel-caption {
  position: absolute;
  left: 15%;
  right: 15%;
  bottom: 20px;
  z-index: 10;
```

```
  padding-top: 20px;
  padding-bottom: 20px;
  color: @carousel-caption-color;
  text-align: center;
  text-shadow: @carousel-text-shadow;
  & .btn {
    text-shadow: none; // No shadow for button
elements in carousel-caption
  }
}
```

To change the size of the text in <h1> and <p>, we make use of the nested rule in LESS:

```
.carousel-caption {
  position: absolute;
  left: 15%;
  right: 15%;
  bottom: 20px;
  z-index: 10;
  padding-top: 20px;
  padding-bottom: 20px;
  color: @carousel-caption-color;
  text-align: center;
  text-shadow: @carousel-text-shadow;
  & .btn {
    text-shadow: none; // No shadow for button
elements in carousel-caption
  }

  .h1 {
    font-size:60px;
  }

  .p {
    font-size:20px;
  }
}
```

One last thing we need to work on is the bottom margin of the navigation bar. In order to change it, open the *navbar.less*:

```
.navbar {
  position: relative;
  min-height: @navbar-height; // Ensure a ↵
  navbar always shows (e.g., without a ↵
  .navbar-brand in collapsed mode)
  margin-bottom: @navbar-margin-bottom;
  border: 1px solid transparent;
...
```

Above we can see that the value for margin-bottom is set by the variable `@navbar-margin-bottom`, which is defined in *variables.less*:

```
@navbar-margin-bottom: @line-height-computed;
```

Just change it to the value that we want. In this example we change it to 1 px:

```
@navbar-margin-bottom: 1px;
```

Save the *variables.less*, compile the *bootstrap.less*, and we are done!

16

AFFIX

As the name implies, Affix keeps a certain part of the page visible at all times, independent from the page scrolls.

We will create a new page to demonstrate how to use Affix. This new page will have two columns: The first column is for the content while the second column contains the menu for navigating that content.

Previously, when we created a page with a multi-column layout, our page scaled down to one column when it is viewed on small displays. This time we will insist on having a two-column layout at all times, including when it is viewed on small screens. We don't want the two columns to be reduced to one column. In order to do that we use `col-xs-10 col-sm-10 col-md-10 col-lg-10` for the first column and `col-xs-2 col-sm-2 col-md-2 col-`

`lg-2` for the second.

The page will look like this:

Figure 16.1

The content consists of four parts, Part 1 to 4, and by using the menu we can navigate to any of those parts.

Here's how we use Affix on our page:

```
<div class="container">
    <div class="row">
        <div class="col-xs-10 col-sm-10 ↵
        col-md-10 col-lg-10">
            <h1 id="p_1">Part 1</h1>
                <p>Text for Part 1...</p>
            <h1 id="p_2">Part 2</h1>
                <p>Text for Part 2....</p>
            <h1 id="p_3">Part 3</h1>
                <p>Text for Part 3...</p>
            <h1 id="p_4">Part 4</h1>
```

```
            <p>Text for Part 4...</p>
        </div>
        <div class="col-xs-2 col-sm-2 ↵
        col-md-2 col-lg-2">
            <ul class="nav nav-pills ↵
            nav-stacked affix">
                <li class="active"><a href= ↵
                "#p_1">Part 1</a></li>
                <li><a href="#p_2">Part 2</a>↵
                </li>
                <li><a href="#p_3">Part 3</a>↵
                </li>
                <li><a href="#p_4">Part 4</a>↵
                </li>
            </ul>
        </div>
    </div>
</div>
```

View on browser: http://bit.ly/p-affix
Download: http://bit.ly/dl-affix

With Affix, when we scroll up and down the page, the menu is always visible and locked in its position.

17

SCROLLSPY

In this chapter we will keep using the page that we worked on when we were learning about Affix.

By using Affix, we have kept the menu visible at all times. It would be nice if as we scroll down the page, our menu not only stays visible but also highlights which menu item that happens to be visible at that very moment.

Let's say we are scrolling down the page. Part 1 of the page has left the screen and Part 2 is visible. We would like our menu to automatically indicate this by highlighting the menu item Part 2 as active. As we scroll down further and Part 3 is now visible, the menu item Part 3 should be highlighted.

That's ScrollSpy. It 'secretly' watches our scrolling activity and behaves accordingly.

How do we use ScrollSpy in our page? It's easy:

First, add the following to the `<body>`:

```
<body data-spy="scroll" data-target=
"#myScrollspy">
```

`#myScrollspy` is the ID we happened to pick. You can pick any ID you like.

Then, we give that ID to the menu that we have:

```
<div class="col-xs-2 col-sm-2 col-md-2 ↵
col-lg-2" id="myScrollspy">
    <ul class="nav nav-pills nav-stacked ↵
    affix">
        <li class="active"><a href="#p_1"> ↵
        Part 1</a></li>
        <li><a href="#p_2">Part 2</a></li>
        <li><a href="#p_3">Part 3</a></li>
        <li><a href="#p_4">Part 4</a></li>
    </ul>
</div>
```

That's it!

View on browser: http://bit.ly/p-scspy
Download: http://bit.ly/dl-scspy

18

TOOLTIP

Bootstrap's Tooltip looks like below:

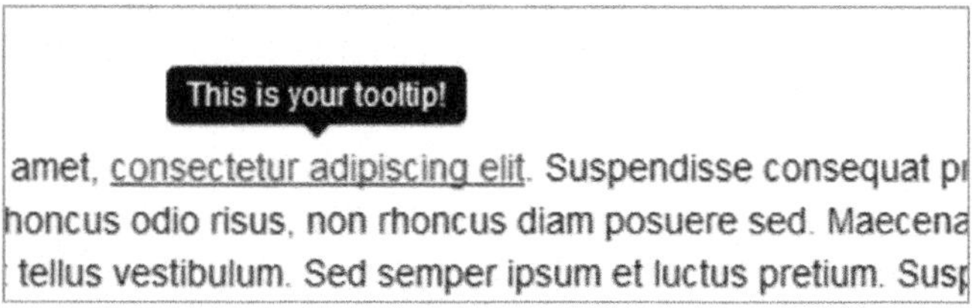

amet, consectetur adipiscing elit. Suspendisse consequat pr
honcus odio risus, non rhoncus diam posuere sed. Maecena
tellus vestibulum. Sed semper ipsum et luctus pretium. Susp

Figure 18.1

To display a Tooltip, add the following into the element that we would like the tooltip to point to:

```
id="[put id here]" data-toggle="tooltip"
    title="[put tooltip text here]"
```

For example, if we would like to display a Tooltip over a hyperlink, we can do:

```
<a href="#" id="tooltipLink" data-
toggle="tooltip" title="This is your
tooltip!">a hyperlink</a>
```

In the above we give our tooltip the ID of *tooltipLink*. Feel free to give any ID you wish.

Unlike other Bootstrap components that we covered previously, for it to work, Tooltip needs to be initialized. In order to do that we need to add a little bit of JQuery. As always, we will place it at the bottom, right after the links to the CDNs.

```
<script src="http://code.jquery.com/jquery-
1.11.1.min.js"></script>
    <script src="http://maxcdn.bootstrapcdn.
    com/bootstrap/3.2.0/js/bootstrap.min.js">
    </script>
    <script>
        $(document).ready(function() {
            $('#tooltipLink').tooltip();
        });
    </script>
...
```

As we can see above, we initialize the tooltip based on its ID (*tooltipLink*). If you use a different ID for the tooltip, just change it accordingly.

The result is as follows:

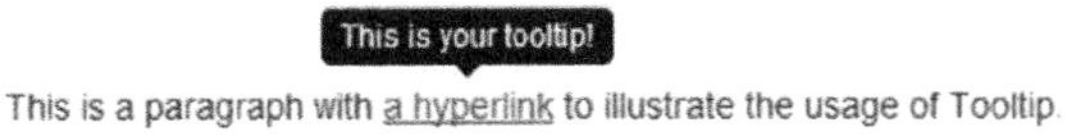

This is your tooltip!

This is a paragraph with a hyperlink to illustrate the usage of Tooltip.

Figure 18.2

View on browser: http://bit.ly/p-ttip
Download: http://bit.ly/dl-ttip

Tooltip can be used on any page element that we want.

For example, we can use it on an image:

```
<img src="image.jpg" id="tooltipImage"
data-toggle="tooltip" title="This is your
tooltip!">
```

Figure 18.3

Or a form:

```
<input type="text" class="form-control"
id="inputName" placeholder="Enter your name"
data-toggle="tooltip" title="This is your
tooltip!">
```

Figure 18.4

18.1 Placement

By default Tooltip will be placed above the element it refers to, as we can see from the examples above.

That does not mean we cannot change its placement. If we want, we can make it to appear to the left, right or bottom of the element. We do this when we initialize the Tooltip:

```
<script>
    $(document).ready(function() {
        $('#tooltipLink').tooltip({
            placement:'bottom'
        });
    });
</script>
```

Or we can set it to *auto* and the Tooltip will be placed dynamically depending on the space. For example if we write `auto right` the Tooltip will be displayed to the right whenever possible. When it is not possible, it will appear to the left.

18.2 Triggers

Triggers are events that cause the Tooltip to appear. The default triggers are *hover* and *focus*, which means the Tooltip will show up if our mouse pointer hovers over the element, or if that page element is in focus.

There are cases where it may be distracting to have Tooltips popping up as we hover around the page. As an alternative, we can change the trigger from *hover* and *focus* to *click*:

```
<script>
    $(document).ready(function() {
        $('#tooltipLink').tooltip({
            trigger:'click'
        });
    });
</script>
```

Or we can choose to control the Tooltip manually. This way we can control the Tooltip from another element.

As an example, we will create a paragraph that has a Tooltip, but this Tooltip will not be displayed when we hover or click on that paragraph. Instead, we will use a button to control it.

Let's create the paragraph and the button:

```
<p id="myHint" data-toggle="tooltip" title= ↵
"This is your hint!">Paragraph content...</p>

<div>
    <button id="btnHint" class="btn btn- ↵
    primary">Show Hint</button>
</div>
```

When we click the *"Show Hint"* button, the Tooltip will appear.

Figure 18.5 shows how the page will look.

Tooltip

Maecenas ac augue dignissim, tincidunt nibh quis, interdum odio. Curabitur tellus dolor, scelerisque vitae libero ac, fringilla vulputate augue. Cras vel convallis enim, non auctor ante. Suspendisse dapibus vel ligula at vehicula. Suspendisse nulla metus, molestie vel malesuada id, porttitor ut arcu. Proin et laoreet leo, blandit accumsan est. Curabitur sit amet nulla in dolor auctor pellentesque. Nullam id odio et nulla tincidunt imperdiet. Morbi ultrices lacinia diam, non porttitor sem dignissim eu. Maecenas et ultricies ipsum.

Show Hint

Figure 18.5

How do we do this? First we initialize the Tooltip and set it to manual:

```
$('#tooltipLink').tooltip({
    trigger:'manual'
});
```

Then we work on the *"Show Hint"* button to give it control over the tooltip:

```
$("#btnHint").click(function(){
    $('#myHint').tooltip("toggle");
});
```

Note:

`toggle` means each time the button is clicked, the Tooltip will be displayed or hidden alternately.

Click the button and we will see:

Figure 18.6

View on browser: http://bit.ly/p-ttipman
Download: http://bit.ly/dl-ttipman

18.3 Using HTML in Tooltip

There will be times when we would like to put an HTML markup inside the Tooltip. A hyperlink, for example. To enable the Tooltip to accept HTML, we have to add the following in the initialization:

```
$('#tooltipLink').tooltip({
    html: 'true'
});
```

To illustrate this, let's reuse the page we created before, with some changes (see the part marked with bold face):

```
<p id="myHint" data-toggle="tooltip"
title="This is your hint!<br><a href='#'>
Click here for more details</a>">Paragraph
content....</p>

<div><button id="btnHint" class="btn
btn-primary">Show Hint</button></div>
```

Change the initialization to include the `html:` `'true'`

```
$('#myHint').tooltip({
    trigger:'manual',
    html:'true'
});

$("#btnHint").click(function(){
    $('#myHint').tooltip("toggle");
});
```

This gives us:

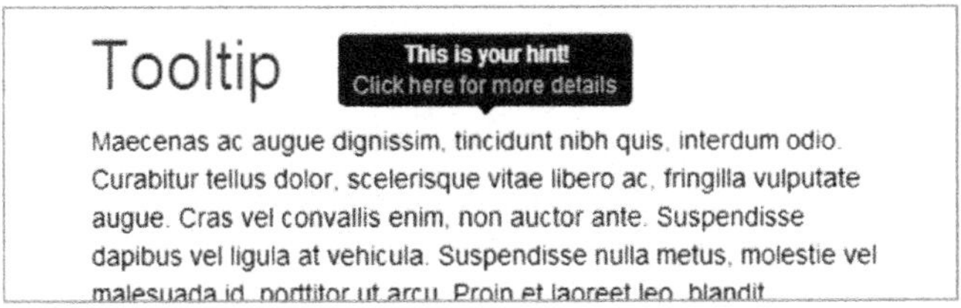

Figure 18.7

View on browser: http://bit.ly/p-ttiphtml
Download: http://bit.ly/dl-ttiphtml

19

POPOVER

Popover is in many ways similar to Tooltip. It works the same way and all the controls that we learned in Tooltip can be used here too.

Below is an example of how to display a Popover on a hyperlink:

```
<p>This is a paragraph with a <a href="#"
id="popoverLink" data-toggle="popover"
title="Popover Title" data-content="The
content of the popover goes here. Feel free
to put a text of any length.">Popover</a>.
As you can see a popover consists of two
parts: the title and the content.</p>
```

Just like Tooltip, Popover needs to be initialized for it to work. We therefore need to add a little bit of JQuery. As always, we will place it at the bottom right after the links to the CDNs.

```
<script>
    $(document).ready(function() {
```

```
      $('#popoverLink').popover();
   });
</script>
```

The Popover will look like this:

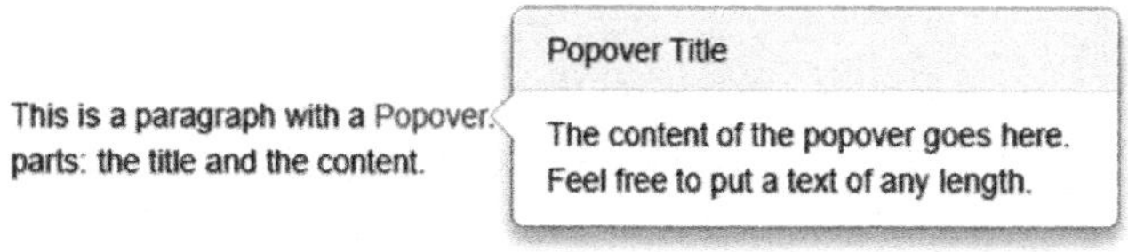

This is a paragraph with a Popover.
parts: the title and the content.

Popover Title

The content of the popover goes here.
Feel free to put a text of any length.

Figure 19.1

View on browser: http://bit.ly/p-pop
Download: http://bit.ly/dl-pop

As seen above, Popover contains two parts: Title and data content. Can we create a Popover without having the title bar on top? Yes we can. Just delete the:

```
title="..."
```

The paragraph becomes:

```
<p>This is a paragraph with a <a href="#"  ↵
id="popoverLink" data-toggle="popover"  ↵
data-content="The content of the popover  ↵
goes here. Feel free to put a text of any  ↵
length.">Popover</a>. As you can see a  ↵
popover consists of two parts: the title  ↵
and the content.</p>
```

And the Popover will be displayed without the title bar:

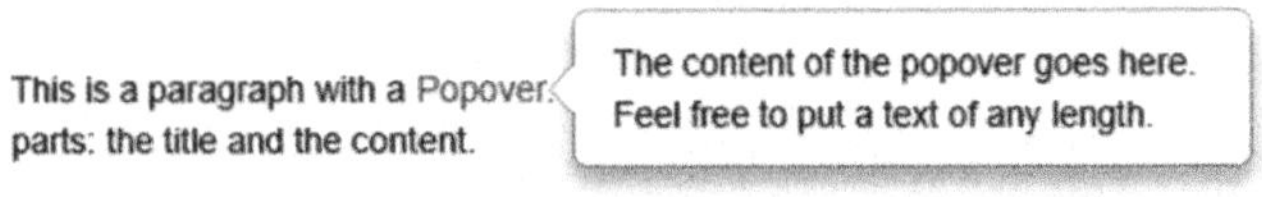

Figure 19.2

View on browser: http://bit.ly/p-popnt
Download: http://bit.ly/dl-popnt

19.1 Placement

The default placement of Popover is on the right of the relevant element. And just like Tooltip, we can change where it will be displayed to anywhere we want to (top, left, or bottom).

```
$('#popoverLink').popover({
    placement:'bottom'
})
```

We can set it to *auto* and the Popover will be placed dynamically depending on the space. For example, if we put `auto-left`, then the Popover will be displayed on the left of the element whenever possible.

19.2 Triggers

The default trigger for Popover is `click`, meaning it will appear when the element containing the Popover is clicked. We can of course change it to *hover*, *focus* or *manual*, just like Tooltip.

```
$('#popoverLink').popover({
    trigger: 'hover'
});
```

19.3 Using HTML in Popover

Just like with Tooltip, to allow HTML to be inserted in the text we do the following at the initialization:

```
$('#popoverLink').popover({
    html:'true'
})
```

Since we can fit a lot more text in Popover, there is a lot more opportunity to use HTML elements inside it. Let's change our paragraph to include some HTML elements. For this example we will add a hyperlink, a list and an image.

```
...
<p>
    This is a paragraph with a  <a href="#"
    id="popoverLink" data-toggle="popover"
    title="Popover Title" data-content="
    <div class='pull-right'>
        <img src='tinyimage.jpg' class='img-
        responsive img-thumbnail'>
    </div>
    <div>The content of the popover goes
    here. Feel free to put a text of any
    length. You can also use HTML markups
    like <a href='#'>hyperlink</a>, a list,
    even adding an image.
        <ol>
            <li>List A</li>
            <li>List B</li>
```

```
        <li>List C</li>
    </ol>
  </div>">popover</a>. As you can see a ↵
  popover consists of two parts: the title ↵
  and the content.
</p>
...
```

Let's initialize the Popover to include HTML. While at it let's set the default placement to below the element:

```
$('#popoverLink').popover({
    html:'true',
    placement:'bottom'
})
```

Figure 19.3

Notice that in this example we also employed Bootstrap's classes inside the Popover. In the above we use the classes `pull-right`, `img-responsive` and `img-thumbnail`, and they work beautifully.

Note:

`pull-right` *is a helper class to float the image to the right. Alternatively you can use* `pull-left` *to float the image to the left.*

View on browser: http://bit.ly/p-pophtml
Download: http://bit.ly/dl-pophtml

20

COLLAPSE

There will be times when we have a lot of information to present on one page. Too much information can overwhelm some readers. One solution would be to keep the page simple by showing only the most important part of the page and hide the rest. When the readers are interested in reading more, he or she can click to display them.

For this we can use Collapse. To illustrate, let's create a page with four paragraphs. Each paragraph has its own title. We name these titles *Parts 1* to *4*. (See figure 20.1)

Our goal is to simplify this page. When opened, we want the page to show only the titles. If the readers are interested in reading more, he or she can click on a title to display the paragraph that corresponds to that particular title.

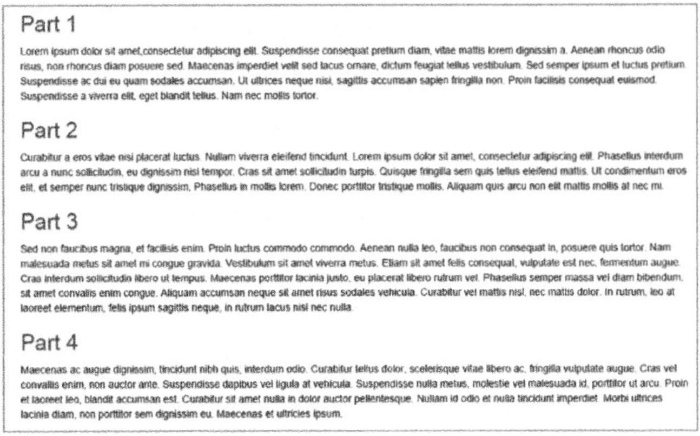

Part 1

Lorem ipsum dolor sit amet,consectetur adipiscing elit. Suspendisse consequat pretium diam, vitae mattis lorem dignissim a. Aenean rhoncus odio risus, non rhoncus diam posuere sed. Maecenas imperdiet velit sed lacus ornare, dictum feugiat tellus vestibulum. Sed semper ipsum et luctus pretium. Suspendisse ac dui eu quam sodales accumsan. Ut ultrices neque nisi, sagittis accumsan sapien fringilla non. Proin facilisis consequat euismod. Suspendisse a viverra elit, eget blandit tellus. Nam nec mollis tortor.

Part 2

Curabitur a eros vitae nisi placerat luctus. Nullam viverra eleifend tincidunt. Lorem ipsum dolor sit amet, consectetur adipiscing elit. Phasellus interdum arcu a nunc sollicitudin, eu dignissim nisi tempor. Cras sit amet sollicitudin turpis. Quisque fringilla sem quis tellus eleifend mattis. Ut condimentum eros elit, et semper nunc tristique dignissim. Phasellus in mollis lorem. Donec porttitor tristique mollis. Aliquam quis arcu non elit mattis mollis at nec mi.

Part 3

Sed non faucibus magna, et facilisis enim. Proin luctus commodo commodo. Aenean nulla leo, faucibus non consequat in, posuere quis tortor. Nam malesuada metus sit amet mi congue gravida. Vestibulum sit amet viverra metus. Etiam sit amet felis consequat, vulputate est nec, fermentum augue. Cras interdum sollicitudin libero ut tempus. Maecenas porttitor lacinia justo, eu placerat libero rutrum vel. Phasellus semper massa vel diam bibendum, sit amet convallis enim congue. Aliquam accumsan neque sit amet risus sodales vehicula. Curabitur vel mattis nisl, nec mattis dolor. In rutrum, leo at laoreet elementum, felis ipsum sagittis neque, in rutrum lacus nisl nec nulla.

Part 4

Maecenas ac augue dignissim, tincidunt nibh quis, interdum odio. Curabitur tellus dolor, scelerisque vitae libero ac, fringilla vulputate augue. Cras vel convallis enim, non auctor ante. Suspendisse dapibus vel ligula at vehicula. Suspendisse nulla metus, molestie vel malesuada id, porttitor ut arcu. Proin et laoreet leo, blandit accumsan est. Curabitur sit amet nulla in dolor auctor pellentesque. Nullam id odio et nulla tincidunt imperdiet. Morbi ultrices lacinia diam, non porttitor sem dignissim eu. Maecenas et ultricies ipsum.

Figure 20.1

```
<div class="container">

    <h1>Collapse</h1>

    <h2><a data-toggle="collapse" href=      ↵
    "#content1">Part 1</a></h2>
    <div id="content1" class="collapse">     ↵
    Paragraph 1...</div>

    <h2><a data-toggle="collapse" href=      ↵
    "#content2">Part 2</a></h2>
    <div id="content2" class="collapse">      ↵
    Paragraph 2...</div>

    <h2><a data-toggle="collapse" href=      ↵
    "#content3">Part 3</a></h2>
    <div id="content3" class="collapse">      ↵
    Paragraph 3...</div>

    <h2><a data-toggle="collapse" href=      ↵
    "#content4">Part 4</a></h2>
    <div id="content4" class="collapse">      ↵
    Paragraph 4...</div>

</div>
```

If we open the page it will look like this:

Part 1

Part 2

Part 3

Part 4

Figure 20.2

Only the titles are displayed. The paragraphs are hidden. When we click on one of the titles, the respective paragraph will be displayed.

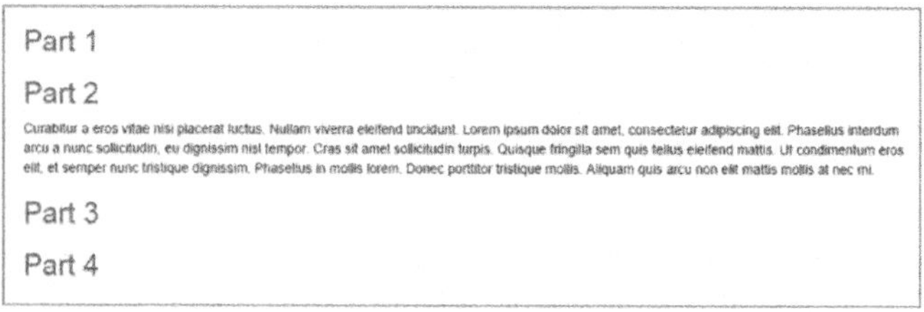

Part 1

Part 2

Curabitur a eros vitae nisi placerat luctus. Nullam viverra eleifend tincidunt. Lorem ipsum dolor sit amet, consectetur adipiscing elit. Phasellus interdum arcu a nunc sollicitudin, eu dignissim nisl tempor. Cras sit amet sollicitudin turpis. Quisque fringilla sem quis tellus eleifend mattis. Ut condimentum eros elit, et semper nunc tristique dignissim. Phasellus in mollis lorem. Donec porttitor tristique mollis. Aliquam quis arcu non elit mattis mollis at nec mi.

Part 3

Part 4

Figure 20.3

Explanation:

We turn the titles into hyperlinks by writing:

```
<a data-toggle="collapse" href="#content1"> ↵
Part 1</a>
```

The href="#content1" determines which part of the page should toggle between being shown or hidden. In this example, it is the part with the ID of *#content1*.

If we click on the title *Part 1*, the content of <div

`id="#content1">...</div>` will be displayed. And if we click it again, it will be hidden.

20.1 Setting a Default

In the example above we start the page by collapsing all paragraphs and showing only the headers. What if we want to have a paragraph that is opened by default whenever we load the page?

It's easy. Add `in` to the following:

```
...
<h2><a data-toggle="collapse" href=
"#content1">Part 1</a></h2>
<div id="content1" class="collapse in">
Paragraph 1...</div>

<h2><a data-toggle="collapse" href=
"#content2">Part 2</a></h2>
<div id="content2" class="collapse">
Paragraph 2...</div>
...
```

Now if we refresh the page, the paragraph of *Part 1* will be shown by default. All other parts are collapsed.

View on browser: http://bit.ly/p-clps
Download: http://bit.ly/dl-clps

20.2 Collapsible Panel

Let's improve the look of our page. We will use

Bootstrap's component called Panel:

Notice the parts we have added that are highlighted in bold face:

```
...
<div class="panel-group" id="accordion">

    <div class="panel panel-default">

        <div class="panel-heading">
            <h2 class="panel-title">
                <a data-toggle="collapse" ↵
                href="#content1">Part 1</a>
            </h2>
        </div>

        <div id="content1" class="collapse">
            <div class="panel-body">
                Paragraph 1...
            </div>
        </div>

    </div>
    ...
</div>
...
```

Part 1
Part 2
Curabitur a eros vitae nisi placerat luctus. Nullam viverra eleifend tincidunt. Lorem ipsum dolor sit amet, consectetur adipiscing elit. Phasellus interdum arcu a nunc sollicitudin, eu dignissim nisl tempor. Cras sit amet sollicitudin turpis. Quisque fringilla sem quis tellus eleifend mattis. Ut condimentum eros elit, et semper nunc tristique dignissim. Phasellus in mollis lorem. Donec porttitor tristique mollis. Aliquam quis arcu non elit mattis mollis at nec mi.
Part 3
Part 4

Figure 20.4

View on browser: http://bit.ly/p-clpsp
Download: http://bit.ly/dl-clpsp

That's better. Except for one small thing: The panel makes it look like we can click anywhere in the area surrounding the title to open the paragraph. But that's not the case. We have to click the title to show or hide the paragraphs. Clicking the gray box will not do anything. Some users may find this frustrating. It would be a lot easier, especially when we are on a mobile device, if we can just click anywhere inside the gray box to see the content.

So let's improve it. This will require a little bit of JQuery.

Notice the changes marked in bold face:

```
<div class="panel panel-default">

    <div class="panel-heading" data-target= ↵
    "#content1">

        <h2 class="panel-title">
            Part 1
        </h2>
    </div>

    <div id="content1" class="collapse">
        <div class="panel-body">
            Paragraph 1...
        </div>
    </div>

</div>
```

Now the titles are no longer hyperlinks. Instead, we put some `data-target` information inside the panel-heading. This information will be read by the JQuery script that is shown below:

```
<script>

    $(document).ready(function() {

        $('.panel-heading').click(function(){
            var target = $(this).data ↵
            ("target");
            $(target).collapse('toggle');
        });

    });

</script>
```

Explanation:

What the script does is whenever an area of `<div class="panel-heading">...</div>` is clicked, it will read the data contained in the `data-target` and use that information as an ID to determine which part should be shown or collapsed.

For example, if we click an area of where the text *Part 1* is, the information inside the `data-target` would be *"#content1"* and the script will use this as an ID to show or collapse the `<div id="content1">...</div>`.

Now we can click anywhere in the gray area to open or hide the paragraphs.

View on browser: http://bit.ly/p-clpspjs
Download: http://bit.ly/dl-clpspjs

20.3 Automatically Collapse Previously Opened Elements

Notice that when we click to open a paragraph, and then we click and open another, the previously opened paragraph remains opened. This means that after some clicking, all paragraphs will be opened and we are back to the problem of having a cluttered screen.

Still in the spirit of keeping our page simple, let's try to do the following:

When we click to open a certain paragraph, the paragraph that was opened previously should automatically collapse. This way the page will only display the content that we are focusing on at that moment.

In order to do this, we need to add a few lines to our JQuery code:

```
<script>

    $(document).ready(function() {

    $('.panel-heading').click(function(){
        var target = $(this).data("target");

        $('#accordion').on('show.bs.collapse'↵
```

```
    , function () {

        $('#accordion .in').collapse ↵
        ('hide');
        });

        $(target).collapse('toggle');
    });
  });

</script>
```

Explanation:

```
$('#accordion').on('show.bs.collapse',
function () {
...
```

When we click on a title, we trigger a command to show a paragraph. The line above is waiting for such a trigger to run the following function:

```
    $('#accordion .in').collapse('hide');
```

In Collapse, when a paragraph is shown, Bootstrap adds a class named `in` to it. The line above makes sure that all that have the class `in` will be hidden.

After all previously opened ones are closed, we will display the content that we selected by using the:

```
        $(target).collapse('toggle');
```

View on browser: http://bit.ly/p-clpsauto
Download: http://bit.ly/dl-clpsauto

20.4 Expand/Collapse All at a Click of a Button

Not everybody will like our keep-it-simple approach. Some would prefer to keep the button clicking to a minimum, and find having to click on each panel to see the details to be cumbersome.

To make sure our site is user-friendly to all, we will cater to this need and create a button to expand or collapse all panels with one click.

Let's put our button under the panels:

```
...
    <div class="panel panel-default">
        <div class="panel-heading"  data- ↵
        target="#content4">
            <h2 class="panel-title">
                Part 4
            </h2>
        </div>
        <div id="content4" class="collapse">
            <div class="panel-body">
                Paragraph 4...
            </div>
        </div>
    </div>
</div>

<div>
    <button class="btn btn-primary" ↵
    id="btnExpandAll">Expand All ↵
    </button>
</div>
...
```

We label this button *Expand All,* and give it the ID of *btnExpandAll.*

To make the button work, we need to add more lines to our JQuery script:

```
<script>
    $(document).ready(function() {
        $('.panel-heading').click(function(){
            var target = $(this).data("target");
            $(target).collapse('toggle');
        });

        $('#btnExpandAll').click(function(){
            $('.collapse').collapse('toggle');

            var label=$('#btnExpandAll').text();
            var newLabel=(label=="Expand All" ↵
            ? "Collapse All" : "Expand All");

            $('#btnExpandAll').text(newLabel);
        });
    });
</script>
```

The page will look like below:

Figure 20.5

And when the button is clicked, all panels will expand, as shown in figure 20.6. The label on the button changes from *"Expand All"* to *"Collapse All"*. If we click on it one more time, the page will return to its original state, where all panels are collapsed and the button's label is changed back to *"Expand All"*.

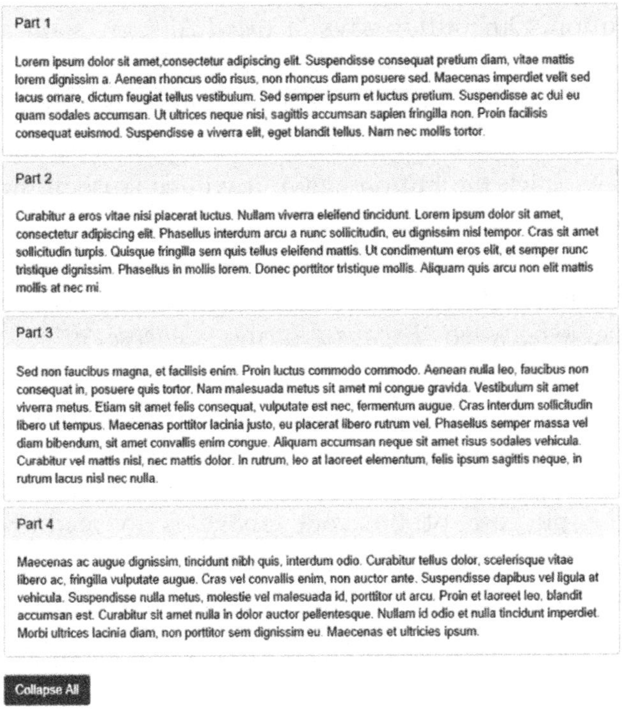

Figure 20.6

Explanation:

When the button *#btnExpandAll* is clicked, we toggle (here it means expand and collapse alternately) all panels that have a class *collapse*. Since all panels have that class, all will expand and collapse at a click of the button.

The rest of the code is dealing with the label of the button. Our button says *"Expand All"*. As soon as we click the button and all panels have been expanded, the words *"Expand All"* is no longer accurate. Now it should say *"Collapse All"*, because if we click the button again, it will collapse all the panels.

We therefore have to make the button's label to toggle between *"Expand All"* and *"Collapse All"*.

```
var label=$('#btnExpandAll').text();
var newLabel=(label=="Expand All" ? ↵
"Collapse All" : "Expand All");
```

The purpose of the code above is to read the button's label and check if the label says *"Expand All"* or not. If yes, it will be changed to *"Collapse All"*. After that, we display the new label on the button:

```
$('#btnExpandAll').text(newLabel);
```

View on browser: http://bit.ly/p-clpsall
Download: http://bit.ly/dl-clpsall

21

PROGRESS BAR

We are all familiar with the Progress bar. We usually see it when a web page is waiting for a process to finish. It could be a file upload, a data retrieval from a database, or a video file conversion, among others.

In most cases, it is the web page (the front end), waiting for a process to be completed on the web server (the back end).

To display a progress bar is easy:

```
<div class="progress">
    <div id="myProgressBar" class="progress-bar" style="width: 25%;"></div>
</div>
```

The width determines the percentage of the progress. In the example above, it is 25%.

It looks like below:

Figure 21.1

Displaying a progress bar statically like this is of course not very useful to us. We need to know how to change the width programmatically, to increase the percentage value to reflect the status of the progress at any given point.

To demonstrate, we will create a button, and whenever this button is clicked, the progress percentage will increase.

When you create your own application you can change the button-click event to the function that you use to obtain the percentage value of the process from the web server. The logic to control the progress bar will remain the same.

Let's create the page:

```
<div class="container">
    <div class="progress">
        <div id="myProgressBar" class= ↵
        "progress-bar" style="width: 0%;"> ↵
        </div>
    </div>
    <div>
        <button class="btn btn-primary" ↵
        id="btnAddProgress">Add progress ↵
        </button>
    </div>
</div>
```

We place the button below the progress bar. We label this button *Add progress*.

Then we add a few lines of JQuery:

```
<script>
    $(document).ready(function() {
        var counter=0;
        var increaseFactor=5;
        $("#btnAddProgress").click(function(){
            counter+=increaseFactor;
            if(counter>100){
                counter=0;
            }
            $("#myProgressBar").css('width', ↵
            counter+'%');
        });
    });
</script>
```

Explanation:

Our button is given the ID of *btnAddProgress*. Whenever this button is pressed, a counter is increased by a factor of 5. If the counter reaches 100, we will reset it back to 0.

The line to update the progress bar is below:

```
$("#myProgressBar").css('width', counter+'%');
```

As we can see above, we increase the width using the value of the counter, so at every click, the progress bar will increase by 5%.

The progress bar and the button will look like this:

Figure 21.2

View on browser: http://bit.ly/p-pbar
Download: http://bit.ly/dl-pbar

21.1 Displaying Percentage Value

If necessary, we can display the percentage value inside the progress bar. In order to do that we need to make a small adjustment in the JQuery code:

```
<script>
    $(document).ready(function() {
        var counter=0;
        $("#btnAddProgress").click(function(){
            counter+=5;
            if(counter>100){
                counter=0;
            }
            $("#myProgressBar").css('width', ↵
            counter+'%');
            $("#myProgressBar").text(counter+↵
            '%');
        });
    });
</script>
```

Our progress bar has the ID of *myProgressBar* and we use that ID to display the text containing the value of *counter* plus the % sign.

The progress bar with the corresponding percentage value displayed will look like below:

Figure 21.3

View on browser: http://bit.ly/p-pbarpct
Download: http://bit.ly/dl-pbarpct

21.2 Changing the Style of Progress Bar

In case we do not like the default style of the progress bar, Bootstrap provides some options:

We can have the bar to in a different color, such as:

Green:

```
class="progress-bar progress-bar-success"
```

Orange:

```
class="progress-bar progress-bar-warning"
```

Red:

```
class="progress-bar progress-bar-danger"
```

We can also add stripes, like this:

Figure 21.4

```
class="progress-bar progress-bar-striped"
```

Or use a color with stripes. Below for example, the bar will be red and with stripes:

```
class="progress-bar progress-bar-success
        progress-bar-striped"
```

We can also animate the stripes, to make it as if they move from the right to the left:

```
class="progress-bar progress-bar-striped
            active"
```

22

SHOW/HIDE PART OF A PAGE BASED ON SCREEN SIZE

There will come a time when we want to display a certain part of the page only when the page is viewed on a certain screen size.

Displaying an advertisement, for example. Some of us may want to display it only when there is plenty of space, such as on a large screen, and refrain from displaying it on a small screen in order to preserve good user experience.

In any case, we need the flexibility to show and hide certain parts of the page when viewed on certain screen sizes.

As an example, let's create a page that contains four different parts, to represent the range of screen sizes: extra small, small, medium and large:

```
<div class="container">

    <h1 class="text-center">Show or Hide ↵
    Based On Screen Size</h1>

    <div class="well">
        <h4>Extra Small Screen</h4>
        <p>Screen size &lt;768px</p>
    </div>

    <div class="well">
        <h4>Small Screen</h4>
        <p>Screen size &gt;=768px and ↵
        &lt;992px</p>
    </div>

    <div class="well">
        <h4>Medium Screen</h4>
        <p>Screen size &gt;=992px and ↵
        &lt;1200px</p>
    </div>

    <div class="well">
        <h4>Large Screen</h4>
        <p>Screen size &gt;=1200px</p>
    </div>

</div>
```

The page is shown in Figure 22.1.

Now we are going to display one part at a time, in accordance with the screen size.

The easiest way to do this is to use the following:

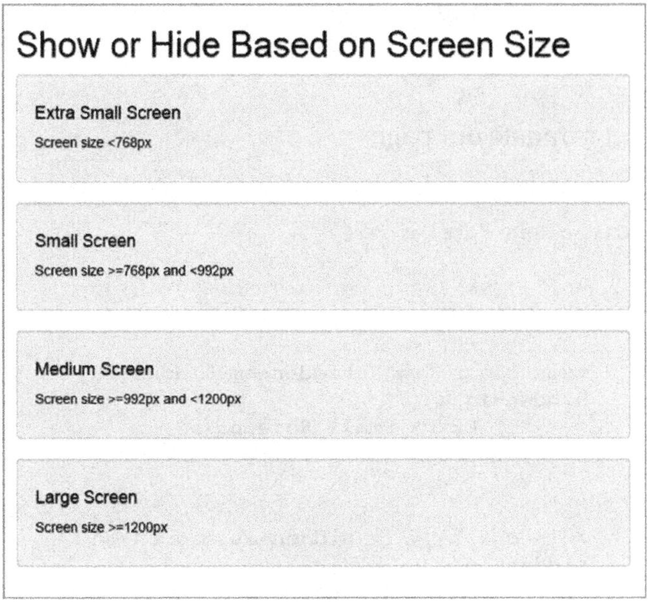

Figure 22.1

hidden-xs:

Do not show on extra small screen (<768px)

hidden-sm:

Do not show on small screen (>=768px and <992px)

hidden-md:

Do not show on medium screen (>=992px and <1200px)

hidden_lg:

Do not show on large screen (>=1200px)

For example, if we want to display the content exclusively on large screens, we write:

```
<div class="hidden-xs hidden-sm hidden-md">
    Content here
</div>
```

Let's update our page:

```
<div class="container">

    <h1 class="text-center">Show or Hide ↵
    Based On Screen Size</h1>

    <div class="well hidden-sm hidden-md ↵
    hidden-lg">
        <h2>Extra Small Screen</h2>
        <p>Screen size &lt;768px</p>
    </div>

    <div class="well hidden-xs hidden-md ↵
    hidden-lg">
        <h2>Small Screen</h2>
        <p>Screen size &gt;=768px and ↵
        &lt;992px</p>
    </div>

    <div class="well hidden-xs hidden-sm ↵
    hidden-lg">
        <h2>Medium Screen</h2>
        <p>Screen size &gt;=992px and ↵
        &lt;1200px</p>
    </div>

    <div class="well hidden-xs hidden-sm ↵
    hidden-md">
        <h2>Large Screen</h2>
        <p>Screen size &gt;=1200px</p>
    </div>

</div>
```

To see it in action, open the page on a computer. Resize the browser window by dragging the corner. See how the page changes as you shrink or expand the page.

Figure 22.2

Figure 22.3

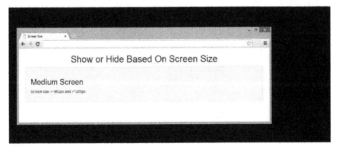

Figure 22.4

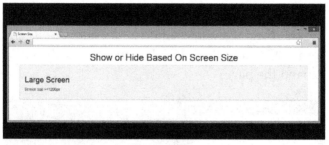

Figure 22.5

View on browser: http://bit.ly/p-show
Download: http://bit.ly/dl-show

Note:

The pixel numbers for the screen sizes (<768px for extra small, >=768px and <992px for small etc) are determined by Bootstrap. It is usually sufficient for our needs, but if you need to change it you can do so through LESS.

The classes `hidden-**` *are defined in responsive-utilities.less. The variables that are used to define the screen size (*`@screen-size-*`*) are defined in variables.less.*

In the example above we also utilized a Bootstrap class that has not been used before. That class is `well`. *We use it to separate the four different contents by giving them extra paddings, a darker background color and rounded borders.*

23

NEXT STEPS

Congratulations! You have finished all the lessons. Hopefully by the time you read this you feel a lot more comfortable with Bootstrap.

This book does not presume to cover everything. Therefore it would be a good idea to talk about the next steps.

Explore Further

There are more components that Bootstrap has to offer than this book can cover. After reading this book make sure you pay a visit to *getbootstrap.com* and explore further. After all the exercises that you have done, it should be easier for you to proceed on your own.

Accessibility

One important aspect that you need to consider and was not covered in this book is web accessibility. It is very likely that there will be some potential visitors to your site who are less fortunate and must rely on the assistance of a screen-reader to browse the web. In this sense, having a website that is readable by screen-readers would be a big help.

One quick example of improving accessibility is by making use of the Role attribute. A button, for example, should be declared to have a role as a button in order to be recognized by screen-readers.

```
<button id="..." role="button"> Button Name ↵
</button>
```

The same goes for Tabs. To be recognized as tabs by screen-readers, the Tabs that we created in Chapter 8 should be written as follows:

```
<ul class="nav nav-tabs">

    <li class="active" role="tab">
        <a href="#">Home</a>
    </li>
    <li role="tab">
        <a href="#">Menu 1</a>
    </li>
    <li role="tab">
        <a href="#">Menu 2</a>
    </li>
    <li role="tab">
        <a href="#">Menu 3</a>
    </li>

</ul>
```

You can research this topic further by typing ARIA

- Accessible Rich Internet Applications on your favorite search engine.

Server-side Programming

Another point that you should be aware of, if you are not by now, is that Bootstrap is all about the front end of the website. If you are only building a prototype or you have programmers to deal with the rest, then you are fine. But if you are planning to build a dynamic website on your own, there are the server-side aspects that you will need to get familiar with.

Think about when we were working on forms and form validations. In the examples presented, when we click the form's submit button, it submits to nowhere. That is because the processing part is usually done on the server side. The data will be submitted from the browser to the server and there will be more validations, access to the database etc. performed by the server. When the process is done, the result is returned to the browser, and displayed as a response. This is a wide subject in itself and therefore cannot be covered in this book.

If you are interested in knowing more about the server-side of web development, try to explore PHP. It is very popular and very easy to learn.

Thank You

Every effort has been made to test and verify all of the information presented in this book. However, it is still possible that mistakes may have been overlooked, versions may change, links to external sites may point to pages that have moved or disappeared altogether. If you notice any errors, or you have any comment or input that can help improve this book, feel free to send it to *riwanto@outlook.com*.

All comments and suggestions will be highly appreciated.

Thank you for purchasing this book and good luck with your website!

Link to download all examples in one zip file:
http://bit.ly/sbsboot_all

APPENDIX 1:
A QUICK INTRODUCTION TO CSS

This appendix is intended to help absolute beginners to get started with Cascading Style Sheet (CSS). If you are already familiar with CSS and how it works, you do not need to read this.

We use CSS to add style to an HTML page. To illustrate its concept, let's start with a plain HTML page:

```html
<!DOCTYPE html>
<html>
    <head>
        <meta charset="UTF-8">
        <title>Introduction to CSS</title>
    </head>
    <body>
        <h1>Introduction to CSS</h1>

        <h2>Title 1</h2>
        <div>Content of Part 1</div>

        <h2>Title 2</h2>
        <div>Content of Part 2</div>

        <h2>Title 3</h2>
        <div>Content of Part 3</div>

        <h2>Title 4</h2>
        <div>Content of Part 4</div>
    </body>
</html>
```

Note:

In our example we use page fillers to beef up the content. We did not display the page fillers in the code above to keep the code simple.

The page looks like this:

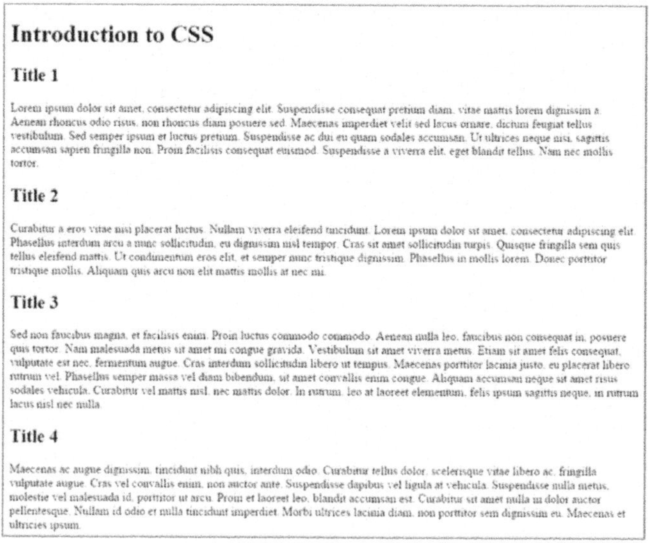

Introduction to CSS

Title 1

Lorem ipsum dolor sit amet, consectetur adipiscing elit. Suspendisse consequat pretium diam, vitae mattis lorem dignissim a. Aenean rhoncus odio risus, non rhoncus diam posuere sed. Maecenas imperdiet velit sed lacus ornare, dictum feugiat tellus vestibulum. Sed semper ipsum et luctus pretium. Suspendisse ac dui eu quam sodales accumsan. Ut ultrices neque nisi, sagittis accumsan sapien fringilla non. Proin facilisis consequat euismod. Suspendisse a viverra elit, eget blandit tellus. Nam nec mollis tortor.

Title 2

Curabitur a eros vitae nisi placerat luctus. Nullam viverra eleifend tincidunt. Lorem ipsum dolor sit amet, consectetur adipiscing elit. Phasellus interdum arcu a nunc sollicitudin, eu dignissim nisl tempor. Cras sit amet sollicitudin turpis. Quisque fringilla sem quis tellus eleifend mattis. Ut condimentum eros elit, et semper nunc tristique dignissim. Phasellus in mollis lorem. Donec porttitor tristique mollis. Aliquam quis arcu non elit mattis mollis at nec mi.

Title 3

Sed non faucibus magna, et facilisis enim. Proin luctus commodo commodo. Aenean nulla leo, faucibus non consequat in, posuere quis tortor. Nam malesuada metus sit amet mi congue gravida. Vestibulum sit amet viverra metus. Etiam sit amet felis consequat, vulputate est nec, fermentum augue. Cras interdum sollicitudin libero ut tempus. Maecenas porttitor lacinia justo, eu placerat libero rutrum vel. Phasellus semper massa vel diam bibendum, sit amet convallis enim congue. Aliquam accumsan neque sit amet risus sodales vehicula. Curabitur vel mattis nisl, nec mattis dolor. In rutrum leo at laoreet elementum, felis ipsum sagittis neque, in rutrum lacus nisl nec nulla.

Title 4

Maecenas ac augue dignissim, tincidunt nibh quis, interdum odio. Curabitur tellus dolor, scelerisque vitae libero ac, fringilla vulputate augue. Cras vel convallis enim, non auctor ante. Suspendisse dapibus vel ligula at vehicula. Suspendisse nulla metus, molestie vel malesuada id, porttitor ut arcu. Proin et laoreet leo, blandit accumsan est. Curabitur sit amet nulla in dolor auctor pellentesque. Nullam id odio et nulla tincidunt imperdiet. Morbi ultrices lacinia diam, non porttitor sem dignissim eu. Maecenas et ultrices ipsum.

Figure A1..1

By default, this page already has a bit of style. The header, as indicated by `<h1>` in the HTML, is displayed larger than the titles (`<h2>`), and the titles are displayed larger than the paragraphs.

Now we are going to add more styles into it.

A1.1 Adding CSS to an HTML page

Let's start by moving the header to the center of the page. There are three ways to do this using CSS:

1. Inline Style

```
...
<body>

        <h1 style="text-align:center;"> ↵
        Introduction to CSS</h1>

        <h2>Title 1</h2>
        <div>Content of Part 1</div>
...
```

2. Internal Style Sheet

```
...
<head>
    <meta charset="UTF-8">
    <title>Introduction to CSS</title>
    <style>
        h1 {text-align:center;}
    </style>
</head>

<body>

    <h1>Introduction to CSS</h1>
...
```

3. External Style Sheet

We create a separate file, let's call it *style.css*, and in it we write:

```
h1 {text-align:center;}
```

Then we link that file to our HTML page:

```
...
<head>
    <meta charset="UTF-8">
    <title>Introduction to CSS</title>
    <link rel="stylesheet" type="text/css"  ↵
    href="style.css">
</head>

<body>

    <h1>Introduction to CSS</h1>
...
```

All three methods will achieve the same objective: Moving the header to the center of the page:

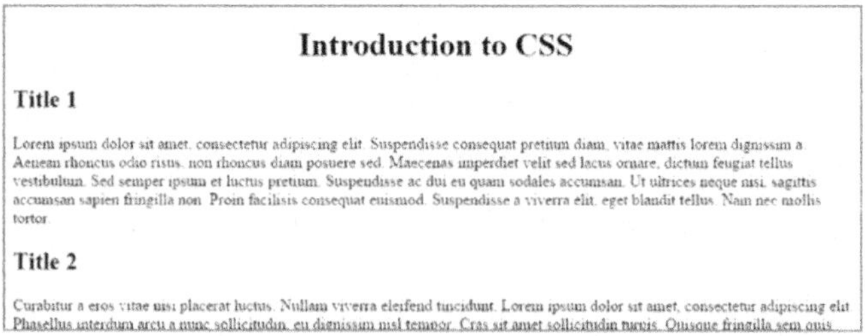

Figure A1.2

View on browser: http://bit.ly/p-css1
Download: http://bit.ly/dl-css1

Inline, internal and external. Which one should we use? The best practice is to use the external style sheet, because it separates the style sheet from the HTML page. This way we can change the style of a website without interfering with its content.

You will see external style sheet being used by Bootstrap throughout this book. In Chapter 2, you will see the following:

```
...
<head>

    <meta charset="UTF-8">
    <title>Welcome</title>

    <link href="bootstrap/css/ ↵
    bootstrap.min.css" rel="stylesheet">

</head>
...
```

Or this:

```
...
<head>
    <meta charset="UTF-8">
    <title>Welcome</title>

    <link href="http://maxcdn. ↵
    bootstrapcdn.com/bootstrap/3.2.0/ ↵
    css/bootstrap.min.css" ↵
    rel="stylesheet">

</head>
...
```

Both are essentially the same: Linking an external style sheet, in this case it is named *bootstrap.min.css*, to an HTML page.

A1.2 Selectors

Let's go back to the style sheet that we have so far:

```
h1 {text-align:center;}
```

What we are doing here is we are 'selecting' h1, and add a style to it. This makes h1 a 'selector'.

In fact, all HTML elements can be selectors. For example, if we want the titles on our page to be displayed in italic, we would do:

```
h2 {font-style:italic;}
```

We can even select the whole page by making <body> a selector. Let's say we would like to give some paddings, margins and borders around our page:

```
body {
    padding:10px;
    margin:20px;
    border:5px solid #888888;
}
```

The page will look like Figure A1.3.

View on browser: http://bit.ly/p-css2
Download: http://bit.ly/dl-css2

A1.2.1 Class Selector

To illustrate the use of a class selector, let's go back

to our HTML page. As we can see, the content of our page has four parts, each has a title and a paragraph:

Figure A1.3

Let's style the paragraph: Give the paragraph some indentation and justify the text alignment.

In order to do that we need to update the HTML page and add the following:

```
<h2>Title 1</h2>
<div class="paragraph">Content of Part 1</div>

<h2>Title 2</h2>
<div class="paragraph">Content of Part 2</div>

<h2>Title 3</h2>
<div class="paragraph">Content of Part 3</div>

<h2>Title 4</h2>
<div class="paragraph">Content of Part 4</div>
```

Then add the following to our *style.css* file:

```
.paragraph {
    text-align:justify;
    text-indent:20px;
}
```

Note the use `class="..."` in the HTML code and the use of . (period sign) to indicate a class selector in the style sheet.

See the result below.

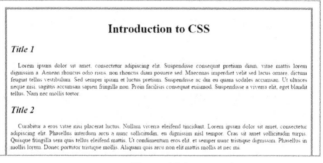

Figure A1.4

View on browser: http://bit.ly/p-css3
Download: http://bit.ly/dl-css3

Explanation:

We create a class called *paragraph,* and put a style in it. Whenever this class is used, that style will be applied.

Throughout this book we see a lot of class selectors being used. For example, in Chapter 3:

```
<div class="container">
    <h1>Hello, welcome to my website!</h1>
    <p>Watch this page grow as we use ↵
    more and more components from ↵
    Bootstrap!</p>
</div>
```

Or in Chapter 7:

```
<div class="container">
    <div class="row">
        <div class="col-md-3">Column 1</div>
        <div class="col-md-3">Column 2</div>
        <div class="col-md-3">Column 3</div>
        <div class="col-md-3">Column 4</div>
    </div>
</div>
```

All of them use class selectors.

A1.2.2 ID Selector

Let's say we would like to put a little more emphasis on our first paragraph. We would like to make it stand out by adding a gray background color and some paddings.

Note that this time we are only targeting the first paragraph. The rest should remain the way it is now.

First, we update the page:

```
...
<h2>Title 1</h2>

<div class="paragraph" id="content1"> ↵
```

```
Content of Part 1</div>

<h2>Title 2</h2>
<div class="paragraph">Content of Part 2</div>

<h2>Title 3</h2>
<div class="paragraph">Content of Part 3</div>

<h2>Title 4</h2>
<div class="paragraph">Content of Part 4</div>
...
```

Then the CSS file:

```
#content1 {
    background-color:#cccccc;
    padding:10px;
}
```

Note the use of `id="..."` In the HTML code and the use of # sign in the style sheet. That indicates that we are using an ID selector.

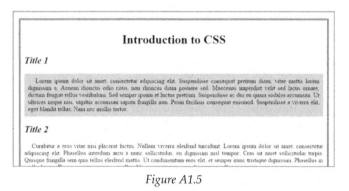

Figure A1.5

View on browser: http://bit.ly/p-css4
Download: http://bit.ly/dl-css4

We use an ID selector to select a specific element.

Unlike a class selector, ID selector has to be unique. No element can share the same ID with another element when they are on the same HTML page.

ID selectors are used a lot in this book too. For example in Chapter 10:

```
...
<div class="modal-fade" id="loginModal" ←
tabindex="-1">

    <div class="modal-dialog">
        <div class="modal-content">
...
```

Or in Chapter 21:

```
...
<div class="container">
    <div class="progress">
        <div id="myProgressBar" class= ←
        "progress-bar" style="width: 0%;"> ←
        </div>
...
```

A1.3 Cascading Order

What happen if we have conflicting styles?

For example, we may write the following:

```
.paragraph {
    text-align:justify;
    text-indent:20px;
    color:red;
}
```

```
#content1 {
    background-color:#cccccc;
    padding:10px;
    color:blue;
}
```

What is going to happen if we use them both like below?

```
<div class="paragraph" id="content1"> ↵
Content of Part 1</div>
```

The paragraph uses both class and ID selectors. The *paragraph* class sets the text color to red, while the ID selector dictates that the text color should be blue. What color would the text be?

CSS has a priority scheme to handle situations like these. The style with higher priority determines what is being displayed. Anything else that the higher priority style does not define will follow either the lower priority or the default style.

One rule in the priority scheme is this: a style applied to HTML via CSS has higher priority than the browser's default style. Remember in the beginning we mentioned that our HTML page already had a style even before we did anything? That is the default style as set by the browser. That style is now overridden by the style we define in our CSS, because CSS has higher priority than browser's default style.

But that does not mean all of the browser's default styles are blocked. The font size, for example, is still using the same size as set in the default style. That is because we never set any font size in our CSS, so the default size 'cascades' down. (Hence the name, cascading style sheet.)

Another important rule in this scheme is this: The more specific selector will win over the less specific one. The ID selector is more specific than the class selector because it pinpoints a specific and unique element. Therefore the ID selector wins.

So to answer the questions above, the text color of our paragraph will not be red. It will be blue, because the ID selector `#content1` has higher priority than the class selector `.paragraph`.

Here's another question: What if both selectors are of equal priority?

Let's say we have this:

```
.paragraph {
    text-align: justify;
    text-indent: 20px;
    color: red;
}
```

And then we write this:

```
.highlight {
    text-align: justify;
    text-indent: 20px;
```

```
    color: green;
}
```

And use them in this:

```
<div class="paragraph highlight" ↵
Content of Part 2</div>
```

Note that both classes are being used. Also note that both selectors are class selectors, and therefore they are of equal priority. The problem is that the two classes have conflicting styles: One set the text color to red, and the other to green. What color will the paragraph be?

The rule in the priority scheme dictates that given everything is of equal priority, the one mentioned last wins.

Since in the style sheet we wrote .paragraph before .highlight, .highlight wins, and our paragraph will be green.

Would it make a difference if we write it like this:

```
<div class="highlight paragraph" ↵
Content of Part 2</div>
```

Instead of this:

```
<div class="paragraph highlight" ↵
Content of Part 2</div>
```

No. What is important is how they are defined in the style sheet. Both lines above are essentially the same. The paragraph will still be green.

A1.4 This is Just the Beginning

You can do a lot more with CSS than what is covered here. This introduction is just your first step into the wonderful world of CSS.

After you are finished with this book and have gained some understanding of how Bootstrap works and how to customize it, and you are off to design your website, you will eventually find yourself relying more and more on your CSS skills than your Bootstrap skills.

CSS is what will enable you to create the wow factor in your designs. Bootstrap is just a framework that speeds up the process.

APPENDIX 2:
A QUICK INTRODUCTION TO LESS

If you look at the downloaded *bootstrap.min.css* file, you will notice that it is quite large: More than 100kB in size. If we print it on letter size (8.5 x 11 in) paper, it can take up to 35 pages.

Maintaining a CSS file that size will not be easy. This is where LESS comes in handy. It helps with the heavy lifting of creating and maintaining the CSS file.

Instead of writing the CSS file directly, we will write it using LESS. This will allow us to use its features that will simplify our work. When we are done, we can compile the LESS file and generate the CSS file.

In short, LESS is a 'CSS maker', or, to borrow the term used in the *lesscss.org* page, it is a CSS pre-processor.

To see how we can benefit from LESS, let's see the following example:

```
.style1 {
    color: #000000;
    background-color:#eeeeee;
    padding:10px;
}
```

```
.style2 {
    color: #000000;
    background-color:#777777;
    padding:10px;
    margin:5px;
}

.style3 {
    color: #000000;
    background-color:#777777;
    padding:10px;
    text-align:center;
    border: 1px solid #333333;
}

#content {
    padding:10px;
    text-align:justify;
}

#content .title {
    font-weight:bold;
    font-size:20px;
}

#content .detail {
    font-size:10px;
}
```

Let's call this our *style.css*. We will now attempt to recreate it by using LESS.

First, we need to create a LESS file. We will call it *style.less*. (Just like CSS, LESS file is a text file, so you can use any text editor to create it.)

Let's start writing our LESS file.

A2.1 LESS Variables

As you can see, our *style.css* contains various values. Values for color, background-color, padding and more. In the future, some of these values may change if we want our site to go with different themes. The way it is written now, whenever there is a need to change any of the values, we will have to go through each of them to make the changes.

It is not a problem if we only have few classes like the above example. Imagine if we have hundreds. It can get tedious.

To make it easier in the future, we can create a LESS file with the following

```less
@black: #000000;
@dark-gray:#333333;
@light-gray:#777777;
@lighter-gray:#eeeeee;

@style-padding:10px;
@style-margin:5px;

.style1 {
    color: @black;
    background-color:@lighter-gray;
    padding:@style-padding;
}

.style2 {
    color: @black;
    background-color:@light-gray;
    padding:@style-padding;
    margin:@style-margin;
```

```
}

.style3 {
    color: @black;
    background-color:@light-gray;
    padding:@style-padding;
    text-align:center;
    border: 1px solid @dark-gray;
}
```

What we did above is replacing all the values with variables, and defining the values of those variables up front. If we compile this file, the output will be exactly the same as the *style.css* we have.

With this technique, whenever we need to make any changes to the value of one of the variables, we only need to go back to our LESS file, find the variable, change the value, compile, and the changes will affect all the classes that use that variable.

A2.2 Mixins

Notice that from *style1* to *style3* there are some repetitions. All of them use the same color and the same size for padding, for example.

Repetition is not a good thing. It is the same work done more than once and we all know that is not efficient. We can improve it by using Mixins.

First, we create a new class containing all the
repetitive parts. Let's name it *black-padded*:

```
.black-padded {
    color: @black;
    padding:@style-padding;
}
```

Then we use this new class as mixins :

```
.style1 {
    .black-padded;
    background-color:@lighter-gray;
}

.style2 {
    .black-padded;
    background-color:@light-gray;
    margin:@style-margin;
}

.style3 {
    .black-padded;
    background-color:@light-gray;
    text-align:center;
    border: 1px solid @dark-gray;
}
```

Let's take it further: In LESS, we can use mixins
inside other mixins. We will use it to tackle another
repetition that still exists above:

```
.black-padded-light {
    .black-padded;
    background-color:@light-gray;
}
```

What we are doing here is we are using the mixins
black-padded to create another mixins: *black-padded-*

light.

Now our style becomes:

```
.style1 {
    .black-padded;
    background-color:@lighter-gray;
}

.style2 {
    .black-padded-light;
    margin:@style-margin;
}

.style3 {
    .black-padded-light;
    text-align:center;
    border: 1px solid @dark-gray;
}
```

Notice how simple our style has become.

A2.3 Nested Rule

Now it is time to tackle the remaining part of our style sheet:

We have the following:

```
#content {
    padding:@style-padding;
    text-align:justify;
}

#content .title {
    font-weight:bold;
    font-size:20px;
```

```
}

#content .detail {
    font-size:10px;
}
```

Using a nested rule, we can transform it into:

```
#content {

    padding:@style-padding;
    text-align:justify;

    .title {
        font-weight:bold;
        font-size:20px;
    }
    .detail {
        font-size:10px;
    }
}
```

A2.4 Operations

Have a look at what we have below:

```
#content {
    padding:@style-padding;
    text-align:justify;
    .title {
        font-weight:bold;
        font-size:20px;
    }
    .detail {
        font-size:10px;
    }
}
```

We set the font size for `title` to be twice the size of the `detail`.

We can do the following:

First, let's create a variable called *content-font-size*:

```
@content-font-size:10px;
```

Then we update the *#content*:

```
#content {
    padding:@style-padding;
    text-align:justify;
    .title {
        font-weight:bold;
        font-size:@content-font-size*2;
    }
    .detail {
        font-size:@content-font-size;
    }
}
```

Now `title` is always twice the size of `detail`. Even better, in the future, if we redesign the page and change the font size of `content` to some other value, the font size of `title` will automatically be twice the new value.

A2.5 Functions

So far we have the following variables:

```
@black: #000000;
@dark-gray:#333333;
@light-gray:#777777;
```

```
@lighter-gray:#eeeeee;
```

Here we are going with a black and white color scheme, using various shades of gray in between. The hexadecimal numbers on the right represent the HTML color codes of each of the grays.

What if we would like to fine-tune our shades of gray? Maybe make one slightly lighter and the other slightly darker?

Without LESS, we would have to find out what the hexadecimal number of the new shade would be and try it out. If we have multiple shades to adjust, it can keep us busy for a while.

Not with LESS. We can do the following:

```
@black: #000000;
@dark-gray:      lighten(@black, 20%);
@light-gray:     lighten(@black, 46.7%);
@lighter-gray:   lighten(@black, 93.5%);
```

The above, when compiled will give us this:

```
@black: #000000;
@dark-gray:#333333;
@light-gray:#777777;
@lighter-gray:#eeeeee;
```

Explanation:

We use the function `lighten` to turn our base color, which is black, into various shades of gray depending on the percentage values.

If we change `lighten(@black, 93.5%)` to 95% for example, we will get the color code `#f2f2f2`. Change it to 100%? Well, that is just turning our black into white (`#ffffff`).

Another benefit of using this function is if we would like to have a different color scheme, say green, we just need to find the green that we want to use as our base, and use it to get the rest of the shades of green.

Let's say we pick the color green `#006600` as our base color. We can do the following to get two shades of lighter green:

```
@green: #006600;
@light-green:   lighten(@green, 15%);
@lighter-green: lighten(@green, 30%);
```

Of course we can do a lot more with LESS's functions than what is described here. The function we used above for example, is just one of the color operation functions. Apart from *lighten* we have *darken*, *fade*, *saturate* and more. LESS also has math functions, string functions and type functions among others.

Below is the final result of our LESS file, in its entirety:

```
@black: #000000;
@dark-gray:     lighten(@black, 20%);
@light-gray:    lighten(@black, 46.7%);
@lighter-gray:  lighten(@black, 93.5%);
```

```less
@style-padding:10px;
@style-margin:5px;

@content-font-size:10px;

.black-padded {
    color: @black;
    padding:@style-padding;
}

.black-padded-light {
    .black-padded;
    background-color:@light-gray;
}

.style1 {
    .black-padded;
    background-color:@lighter-gray;
}

.style2 {
    .black-padded-light;
    margin:@style-margin;
}

.style3 {
    .black-padded-light;
    text-align:center;
    border: 1px solid @dark-gray;
}

#content {
    padding:@style-padding;
    text-align:justify;
    .title {
        font-weight:bold;
        font-size:@content-font-size*2;
    }
    .detail {
        font-size:@content-font-size;
    }
}
```

To learn more about LESS, pay a visit to its site:

`http://lesscss.org`

To read about the language features, go to:

`http://lesscss.org/features/`

To see the list of functions available, go to:

`http://lesscss.org/functions/`

APPENDIX 3:
COMPILING LESS

In order to compile LESS we will need a compiler. If you search using the keyword "LESS compiler" on your favorite search engine, you will find numerous LESS compilers available on the market. CodeKit, WinLess, SimpLESS, Crunch, to name a few. Some are free, some are not. Feel free to choose the one that you like the best.

In this book we will use *Crunch*, simply because *Crunch* is free and runs on multiple platforms.

To download Crunch go to its site:

```
http://crunchapp.net
```

Note:
Crunch will require Adobe AIR to run so make sure you download that too.

Once you are done with all the installations, open Crunch and let's get started.

A3.1. Compiling a LESS File

We will try to compile the style sheet that we created in Appendix 2.

Start by clicking New LESS file:

Figure A3.1

A blank worksheet will open and we can start typing in our LESS.

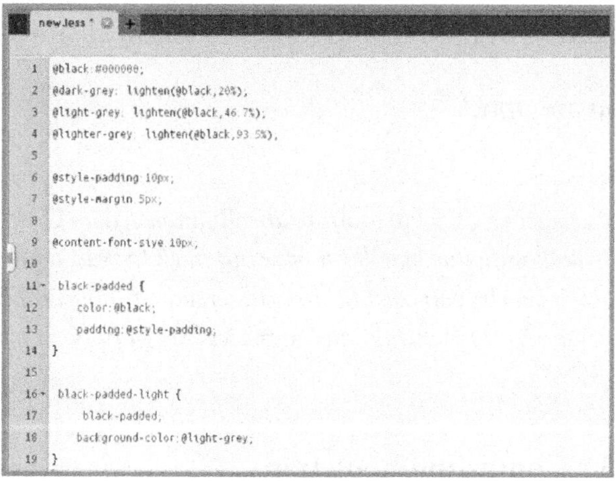

```
1   @black:#000000;
2   @dark-grey: lighten(@black,20%);
3   @light-grey: lighten(@black,46.7%);
4   @lighter-grey: lighten(@black,93.5%);
5
6   @style-padding:10px;
7   @style-margin:5px;
8
9   @content-font-size:10px;
10
11  black-padded {
12      color:@black;
13      padding:@style-padding;
14  }
15
16  black-padded-light {
17      black-padded;
18      background-color:@light-grey;
19  }
```

Figure A3.2

Once we are done, click Save. Crunch will ask you

223

to select the destination folder and the file name. Save the file as *style.less*.

After the file is saved, the Crunch button on the upper right side will be enabled. This is the button that we will use to compile the LESS file.

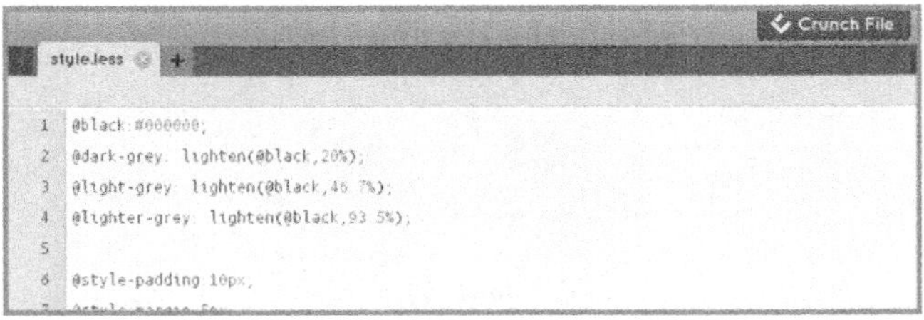

Figure A3.3

Click it. Crunch will ask you to select the destination folder and file name for the CSS file resulting from the compile. Let's name it *style.css*.

You are done!

Note:
The resulting CSS file is automatically minified by Crunch. This makes the file smaller in size but hard to read with the naked eye. If you would like to create a non-minified version, go to Setting and deselect "Minify Crunched CSS".

A3.2 Compiling Bootstrap

In addition to compiling a LESS file that we created ourselves, we should also know how to compile

Bootstrap's source code.

First, download Bootstrap's source code if you have not done so. Unzip the downloaded file and you will get a folder structure like below:

Figure A3.4

At this point we are only interested in the LESS source code stored in the *less* folder.

Drag the whole *less* folder and drop it on the Crunch screen. A folder *less* will show up on the left pane.

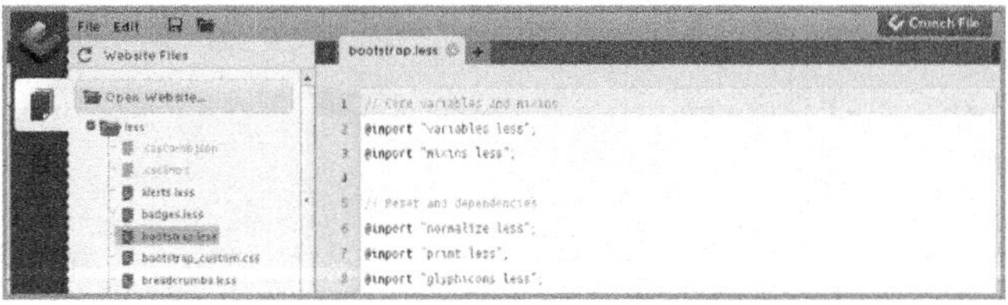

Figure A3.5

Inside you will find all of Bootstrap's LESS file. Click open `bootstrap.less`. Once it is opened, the

Crunch button on the upper right side should become enabled. If you click it, Bootstrap's LESS file will be compiled and a new css file will be generated.

You can of course use Crunch to make changes to Bootstrap's LESS files. For example, if you are going to do the customization work laid out in Chapter 14, you can use Crunch to open the *variables.less* and *jumbotron.less* and work on the changes. Once you are done, find the *bootstrap.less* file again and click the Crunch button to compile it. All of your changes will be incorporated in the resulting CSS file.

INDEX

Made in the USA
Middletown, DE
05 March 2020